The
Practical
Psychic

The Practical Psychic

A NO-NONSENSE GUIDE TO
Developing Your Natural Intuitive Abilities

NOREEN RENIER
PSYCHIC DETECTIVE

adamsmedia
AVON, MASSACHUSETTS

Published by
Adams Media, a division of F+W Media, Inc.
57 Littlefield Street, Avon, MA 02322. U.S.A.
www.adamsmedia.com

ISBN 10: 1-4405-0623-X
ISBN 13: 978-1-4405-0623-9
eISBN 10: 1-4405-0964-6
eISBN 13: 978-1-4405-0964-3

Printed in the United States of America.

10 9 8 7 6 5 4 3 2 1

Library of Congress Cataloging-in-Publication Data
is available from the publisher.

Readers are urged to take all appropriate precautions before undertaking any how-to task. Always read and follow instructions and safety warnings for all tools and materials, and call in a professional if the task stretches your abilities too far. Although every effort has been made to provide the best possible information in this book, neither the publisher nor the author are responsible for accidents, injuries, or damage incurred as a result of tasks undertaken by readers. This book is not a substitute for professional services.

This publication is designed to provide accurate and authoritative information with regard to the subject matter covered. It is sold with the understanding that the publisher is not engaged in rendering legal, accounting, or other professional advice. If legal advice or other expert assistance is required, the services of a competent professional person should be sought.

—From a *Declaration of Principles* jointly adopted by a Committee of the American Bar Association and a Committee of Publishers and Associations

Many of the designations used by manufacturers and sellers to distinguish their product are claimed as trademarks. Where those designations appear in this book and Adams Media was aware of a trademark claim, the designations have been printed with initial capital letters.

This book is available at quantity discounts for bulk purchases.
For information, please call 1-800-289-0963.

Dedication

To all my fans who wanted this book written so they, too, could use their psychic ability to help themselves and others.

Acknowledgments

I wish to express my deepest gratitude to my dear friend, Jim Purks, a former police reporter and Associated Press newsman, now a deacon in the Episcopal Church, for his moral support and encouragement.

I want to thank Shirley Schenkel, friend and author of the delightful, humorous, action-packed Acey Tapp mystery series, whose energy and enthusiasm inspired me.

I thank Dale E. Graff, MS, Physics, for writing the foreword to this book and for always believing in me. Dale is a former director of the United States government's Project Stargate, which researched and applied remote viewing for military intelligence and operational missions. His books include *Tracks in the Psychic Wilderness* and *River Dreams*.

I also want to express my appreciation to my other friends who made important suggestions and contributions: Ellen Burns, Karl Petry, Candy Hood-Levy, Dr. David E. Jones, and Dr. William Roll.

A very special thanks to my publisher, Adams Media, and especially Andrea Norville.

And last, but far from least, my wonderful editor, Skye Alexander.

Contents

Foreword

In *The Practical Psychic: A No-Nonsense Guide to Developing Your Natural Intuitive Abilities*, Noreen Renier succinctly presents what she has learned during thirty years of experience. Her progression from being a skeptic about the existence of psychic talents to being a highly sought-after psychic detective is inspiring, and sends a clear message about the reality and the value of our psychic (psi) talents.

The book clearly explains how we can become aware of psychic information through direct mind-to-mind contact (telepathy), accessing information associated with objects (psychometry), describing distant locations in both space and time (remote viewing, distant seeing), and various kinesthetic methods such as dowsing. Some chapters focus on specific applications, such as psychic criminology, intuitive state-of-health diagnostics, and locating missing or lost people or objects. Noreen describes methods for visualization, memory recall improvement, and meditation/relaxing, because these are key factors in how we can enhance our ordinary cognitive sensitivities and our psychic abilities.

The good news is that psychic talents exist. And even better news is that these psychic talents can be available to anyone. This guidebook is actually an invitation that offers you the opportunity to begin an exciting, life-changing, life-enhancing journey that not only can be of immense value for you, but also for the holistic well-being of everyone in our global community. So enjoy your journey of discovery and be open to the surprises that you will encounter.

Dale E. Graff

Why Psychic Abilities Matter

"Don't ask yourself what the world needs, ask yourself what makes you come alive and then go and do that. Because what this world needs is people who have come alive."

—Harold Whitman

Awareness. Knowing. Insight. Foresight. These are gifts your intuitive senses offer if you learn how to use your brain in a different way, and to explore its vast areas of untapped potential. If you don't, these exciting gifts could go unopened for a lifetime.

Extra Sensory Perception (ESP) means obtaining information or knowledge not with the five human senses (sight, sound, taste, touch, and smell), but with the mind.

My main purpose in writing this book is to answer the question, "If psychic ability exists, how can we use it?" I don't address the technical nature of ESP here, but instead want to share its practical applications. We don't need to understand how our computers, microwaves, or vehicles with all their intricacies work to use them. It's the same with ESP.

Throughout this book, I will show you how to extend the capabilities of your five basic senses and empower you to find new ways of perceiving information. Some of the concepts presented are simple and astonishingly easy. Others are more difficult to understand and master. Practice is essential. So is commitment. But wonderful discoveries await you as you develop your own psychic abilities. The universe will forever offer up new resources, gifts, and adventures for you to discover, develop, and put to meaningful use.

Mysteries Revealed

Not very long ago, we knew little about electricity. Today it's used worldwide and taken for granted, not because everyone understands what it is and how it works, but because we're eager to harness its gifts. Electricity powers our towns and cities, our hospitals, homes, shopping malls, and workplaces. We couldn't function without it. For most of us, electricity will remain a mysterious force but one for which we are thankful.

Your psychic intuition is another unknown, another resource with enormous promise, a promise that you can bring to light. Like electricity, it's a force of nature, but one that usually remains untapped and hidden. I would like to help you tap this resource, tame it, and tune it so it becomes as much a part of who you are as your other five senses.

Why Listen to Me?

Who am I? I am a psychic detective. It has been said publicly, many times, that I'm a good one. I believe I am. In fact, I know I am. I embrace my avocation with enthusiasm, and I practice it with integrity.

I've been called "the most credible psychic out there" by Court TV online. I've worked with law enforcement agencies in thirty-eight states and six foreign countries, and provided information in more than 600 criminal cases, which helped lead law enforcement authorities, crime victims, and distressed individuals and families to answers.

I was the first psychic ever to work with the FBI—and I have taught at the FBI academy in Quantico, Virginia.

I've worked primarily on missing persons and homicide cases. Some of the cases I'm involved in make newspaper headlines, radio broadcast reports, television, and Internet news. Far more do not. Although I am immensely gratified when my work leads to breakthroughs in unsolved crimes—some of them horrendous—I don't seek recognition and praise. I'm appreciative and grateful when it is accurately extended, but that's not why I do the work.

Most law enforcement authorities prefer that I remain behind the scenes and avoid media attention during the investigations. That's okay with me. The truth is, it's easier for me that way. When putting my psychic abilities to work, the fewer distractions, the better. My reward is seeing a case solved, justice served, and people who have been hurt afforded some peace, some closure.

During my career as a psychic detective I have held blood-stained earrings, wallets, watches, shirts, shoes, and other possessions of murder victims. I have psychically sensed the images, feelings, and sensations that reside in such items. My mind taps into the turbulent energy left behind, the energy that lingers from a moment of explosive violence. I have relived the brutal events—their emotions, sights, sounds, smells, and sensations.

How My Work Helps

Psychic detectives like me use their developed awareness, their caring instinct for others, and a sensitive part of their minds to assimilate information and visual impressions about unsolved crimes. This information and these impressions often prove highly valuable to investigators.

Is what I do heroic or special? Some people think so. Others think it's eerie or unnatural. I certainly don't feel heroic or special. And what I do is not eerie or unnatural. To the contrary: it's normal and natural, and something you can do, too.

From my perspective, the real heroes and heroines are the law enforcement officers who work so hard. They toil for long, tedious hours, often in harm's way, to prevent or solve crimes and bring about justice. I especially appreciate those with the vision and courage to go the extra mile necessary to solve a case. Sometimes that means conceding that modern, sophisticated, and high-tech investigative methods have been exhausted and that it's time to seek assistance from an unconventional source, such as a psychic detective. A psychic detective often presents a new perspective or some information that, when interpreted and pursued, brings about a breakthrough in a difficult case.

From Skeptic to Believer

Years ago, I did not believe in people like me. I pooh-poohed all the achievements and phenomena I just described. "No way!" I said to myself. "Psychic phenomena? You've got to be kidding!"

Because I was a skeptic, I understand the skepticism that greets many discussions of what I do now. You'll encounter some of this skepticism within yourself at times, and often from other people as well. Don't be discouraged. Maintain your commitment and your integrity.

As someone who has shown the courage and desire to discover more about yourself and your potential, you, too, should be considered heroic. You're on the threshold of learning to utilize another part of your mind and your gifts in day-to-day situations. You've taken the first step to using your mind in a deeper, different way than you have been taught in school, in the workplace, in the home, and in our society. What an adventure you are about to embark upon!

Understanding and Exploring the Psychic Experience

Do you have psychic potential? Do you possess abilities that you fail to recognize or act on because you're reluctant to accept them as possibilities? Can you really learn to develop and use these abilities to enrich your everyday life? The answer to all three questions is *yes*. Many of the world's greatest geniuses, including Albert Einstein and Leonardo da Vinci, admitted to relying on more than just their rational minds for guidance and inspiration. Einstein even stated, "The only real valuable thing is intuition." Thomas Edison, Harry Truman, and Benjamin Franklin were known to sleep on it when confronted with an important decision, in order to gain wisdom from their dreams. You, too, can access the potential that lies within your intuitive mind to solve problems, improve your relationships with other people, and walk your path in life more gracefully.

Uncovering Your Potential

You are psychic. We all are. Those sudden hunches, curious dreams, recurring thoughts, and flashes of insight that you experience come from a source that you can learn to interpret, control, and use for good—not only for yourself, but also for the world.

Sadly, we have been conditioned to ignore it or deny it. Due to ignorance or superstition, we may even fear it. But it's there—to be used for good, for communication, for growth, for healing, and for happiness.

A Bias Toward Logic

Our cultural hang-ups have handcuffed us with intimidating words such as, "that's not logical" or "that doesn't compute." Our society considers it normal to use only a small portion of the mind and to accept the objective, material realm as the "real" world. This helps to bring about uniformity and conformity. It makes us more comfortable. Early in life, we were trained to emphasize the logical, rational part of the mind. Our fascination with high-tech toys illustrates this tendency. Encouraging and rewarding the logical, rational, thinking mind has carried our civilization a long way.

But these technological advances have come at the expense of the intuitive mind. As a result, within each of us lies a vast, unknown, and barely charted territory. Even though we know creativity, dreams, and intuitive leaps spring from the "irrational" part of the brain, our educational system and science in general tend to neglect this resource or deny its existence. Yet it's there: a dimension of loving power that most of us have either pushed aside or tried to avoid, like a friend who embarrasses us, whom we wish would go away.

We need to harness both the rational and irrational parts of our brains to achieve our full potential. We need reason and inspiration, logic and intuition, words and feelings, numbers and images.

My goal in writing this book is to help you develop your psychic abilities and bring them up to par with your reasoning powers. Collaboration is part of human nature. We have two hands so that each can help the other work more productively, two eyes to broaden our view, two ears to hear the music of the world around us—and two brains to function optimally in life. Why settle for half a brain when you can reap the benefits of the whole thing?

Embracing the Intuitive Mind

I'm frequently asked, "How does ESP work?" I reply, "You have been using your logical, rational, analytical mind for years . . . how does it work?"

Think back to your childhood. Your parents didn't explain how your thinking mind worked when you started school, but they encouraged you. They expected you to learn to add, subtract, multiply, divide, read, spell, and speak in complete sentences. They believed you could do it; they made you believe you could do it. You had to practice, you did homework—but you certainly didn't understand how your brain worked in order to use it. Most of us still don't.

Often, we hear intuition's quiet voice speaking to us in the form of a physical or emotional feeling we can't explain. Or it nudges us in a dream that won't let go and provokes us to delve deeper. Sometimes the intuitive mind speaks so loudly and with such insistence we can't ignore it.

When I teach classes in ESP, I always ask my students to leave their rational minds at the door. Skeptics have criticized me for this. They twist my words and allege that I am urging people to ignore their critical faculties and blindly accept everything I tell them. Nothing could be further from the truth. My objective—like a parent who encourages her child to learn and excel in school—is to guide you in strengthening your psychic ability. You don't have to know all the specifics about how your intuitive mind works, you just have to believe in your powers and commit to improving them.

We seek balance in life, and that includes bringing the rational mind and the intuitive mind into parity. Many law enforcement officers who have worked with me have learned to respect their own gut feelings just a little bit more. At the same time, they have retained, if not sharpened, their own analytical and attention-to-detail natures. My work with them has taught me to respect their ability to stick closely to facts, refusing to be swayed by tall stories and con artists.

You may doubt that you have untapped psychic abilities. Although the skill may be new to you, it exists. Have no doubt about that. You can find it, access it, and use it. Using this psychic resource calls for commitment and trust—in me and in the guidance offered in this book, but above all, in yourself. An expanded, deeper, and more complete awareness lies within your grasp. It offers excitement, fun, fulfillment, and a pathway to joyfully thriving in our incredibly fast-paced universe.

Think about the different times you've tackled something new. Most likely, you've been excited and hopeful. Now you have the opportunity to put that same energy, hope, and excitement for the future into exploring your psychic abilities. I believe that you have the capacity to thrive in this high-tech, high-energy twenty-first century. Physically. Psychically. Emotionally. Spiritually. Practically. Come, journey with me.

CHAPTER 1

Enhancing Your Awareness Through Meditation

"Meditation brings wisdom; lack of meditation leaves ignorance."
—The Buddha

Developing your psychic abilities requires training your awareness. One of the best ways to do this is through meditation. Meditation is a state of deep relaxation during which mental chatter ceases temporarily and you become wholly present in the moment. However, it's more than a process of reflection or contemplation. It is more than visualization, daydreaming, or relaxation. Your brainwave frequencies slow down from 13–30 cycles per second (your everyday level of consciousness) to about 8–13 cps (the intuitive level).

Meditation involves training your mind to stop jumping about like a monkey in a tree and grow quiet. You yield the desire or need to control everything, and surrender your body and mind so the still, small voice inside can share its wisdom with you. This process of concentration-control-surrender is a structured, guided approach to self-development that carries the added benefits of enhancing physical, emotional, and psychological well-being.

The Benefits of Meditation

Meditation can lower your blood pressure, soothe your nervous system, ease anxiety, and slow your heartbeat and breathing rate. Many studies show that meditation can help those suffering from conditions such as diabetes, coronary disease, cancer, chronic pain, and others. More than 240 hospitals and medical facilities now offer meditation programs—even the U.S. military is exploring meditation for treating post-traumatic stress disorder. Those are just a few of the physical benefits—but there are others as well.

Meditation stills the mind, and that stillness allows you greater contact with the intuitive part of your brain. When you draw upon both the rational and the intuitive parts of your brain, you become more creative, inspired, and productive.

That's why corporations such as Apple Computer, Yahoo, and Google offer meditation classes to their employees. In fact, a UCLA study published in 2009 found that meditation actually increases the size of the brain. Another study conducted at Massachusetts General Hospital in 2005 showed that meditation improved decision-making, attention, and memory.

Because meditation reduces stress, it produces an increased sense of tranquility. When inmates at six Massachusetts prisons practiced meditation in 2007, hostility declined and self-esteem improved. You, too, can obtain inner peace from meditation, and your newfound serenity can inspire others. You can be an instrument of change in the universe.

Dealing with Distractions

Meditation done right is especially hard in our go-go-go culture, where achievement and climbing the success ladder are top priorities. For many people, being still feels very uncomfortable. Introspection also makes us uneasy. Instead, we prefer to turn our attention outward and seek distractions that keep us from looking too deeply within ourselves. Distractions are rampant. The cell phone rings, or a signal tells us there's an insistent text message we must answer. The TV bombards us with constant chatter and images.

It doesn't matter if you're at home, at work, on a hike in a beautiful area, or in a sacred space: you won't find peace unless you make a deliberate commitment to meditate. As many spiritual traditions and teachers advise, meditation can help you find out just who you really are, what your potential is, and how you can positively contribute to this world. Set aside time every day to meditate, even if it's only ten minutes. Turn off the phone, the TV, the radio. Put a Do Not Disturb sign on the door. Make meditation a priority in your life—you'll soon notice all sorts of benefits.

Meditation and Intuition

When done right, meditation nudges aside external distractions. It muffles mental chatter and allows you to turn inward. Your breathing deepens and your mind becomes still. Because the noise has been silenced, you can receive insight and guidance from the part of your mind that you may not listen to regularly. Gradually that part of the brain says, "Here I am."

Meditation lets you connect with the intuitive part of your brain and use its capabilities more fully. With the help of meditation, a developed psychic awareness can begin to unfold. You can enhance opportunities that have always been present and bring your innate powers to fulfillment.

The First Stages of Meditation

In the first stages of meditation, you'll experience increased relaxation and awareness. As your awareness becomes keener and more sensitive, you'll begin to perceive things you might not have noticed before. As your mental clutter clears, you'll receive more insights and information from your intuition. These are the first steps to realizing your psychic ability. But don't expect instant gratification. Commitment and practice are needed to develop your ability.

Think Positive

Through regular meditation, you'll learn to control your thoughts. How you project your thoughts creates your reality.

We've all seen the pattern. A person whose thoughts and beliefs are negative often has a life filled with obstacles, sickness, and pain. On the other hand, a person who cultivates thoughts of love, peace, understanding, and forgiveness attracts positive people and experiences. Certainly, we all face challenges, adversity, and setbacks. And it's true that bad things do happen to good people. But as countless spiritual teachers and motivational speakers have expressed, maintaining a positive outlook—seeing the glass as half-full rather than half-empty—can help you live a happier, healthier life. Meditation trains your mind and makes it easier for you to shift your thinking to a more positive track.

Listen to Your Intuition

As you progress and stay true to your commitment to meditate regularly, you'll start listening more often to the intuitive part of your brain. You'll start to receive insights while meditating. Here's an example. Let's say you have a health concern. When you sit down to meditate, ask your inner knowing to provide information that will help you deal with this matter. As you grow mentally and physically relaxed, an impression of a remedy, treatment, or practice that can benefit you may pop into your mind—perhaps something you hadn't considered before.

When your intuitive mind presents guidance, answers, and information during meditation, pay attention. These "aha" insights might come to you as words, pictures, or feelings. Write down these epiphanies after you come out of meditation. Notice how they apply to situations in your everyday life. These insights may even alert you to something that will happen in the future.

This happens partly because your intuition can finally get through to you once your mind stops racing like a hamster in a treadmill. It's also because meditation strengthens the part of your brain associated with intuitive functioning. You continue to hear what your logical brain says, but with the added abilities of the intuitive/emotional side of the brain, you can more sensitively and accurately discern what's going on around you. You *feel* what's right or wrong. You learn to trust your gut response as well as your rational thinking.

We've all made decisions that go against reason. How many times have you sensed that something wasn't right? Or felt bodily uneasiness, sweating, or a prickly feeling? How many times, after ignoring or refusing to believe an intuitive message, have you ruefully said to yourself, "I knew I shouldn't have done that" or "I knew I should have taken the other way" or "I knew s/he wasn't right for me"?

Intuition and psychic awareness constantly transmit signals and information that can help us take advantage of opportunities or prevent mishaps.

In my classes, I'm frequently asked, "What if I misinterpret an intuitive feeling? What if I make a mistake?" I respond that we're not perfect. We're human. We make mistakes when we use our logical minds, too. We learn from our mistakes. As with any skill, the more we use our intuition, the better we become at it and the stronger our sixth sense grows. The old saying "practice, practice, practice" applies here as it does in every area of life. The more we tap in to our psychic awareness and abilities, the more we'll grow as people and as positive forces in the world.

Awakening Your Psychic Powers

Over time, as you continue meditating and working with more of your brain, your understanding of the world and the way you experience life will change. When you walk down the street, ride the subway or bus, and sit at your desk or at the kitchen table, your outlook will be shifting. Along with using more of your brain—or at least becoming more clear about what it's conveying to you—you will experience a heightened awareness of things beyond the mundane, material world you've been used to up till now.

- You may notice synchronicities—meaningful coincidences —occurring more frequently.
- You may begin to sense things before they happen.
- You may feel the pace of your life speed up or slow down.
- Your dreams may become more meaningful.
- You may feel more compassionate, more accepting, or more connected to the people in your life—and more willing to assist them.
- You may become aware of possibilities and opportunities whizzing around you.
- You may sense things about people and situations, past and future, that you *shouldn't* know, at least according to logic.

Not surprisingly, you may be a bit confused or overwhelmed as you adjust to a different understanding of reality. You'll probably find yourself asking the universe for help in situations you might previously have attempted to handle alone. But don't worry, control will come. You are embarking on a fantastic journey. Relax, trust, and enjoy the process.

BREATHING MEDITATION

Observing your breath is an easy and popular meditation technique. Without actively influencing your breath, just sit quietly and become aware of your breathing.

1. Sit in a comfortable position with your eyes closed. (It's best not to lie down; you might get too relaxed and fall asleep.)
2. Pay attention to your breathing. Notice how your abdomen and chest expand as you inhale, and deflate as you exhale.
3. Listen to your inhalations and exhalations, without analysis.

Observe your breathing in this manner for two to three minutes at least once a day. The goal is simply to keep your attention on your breathing. This basic form of meditation relaxes and balances your body, mind, and spirit.

Different Types of Meditation

Usually the word *meditation* calls to mind images of a yogi sitting cross-legged in the lotus position and chanting *oooohhhhmmmm*, but that's only a small part of the picture. Many different types of meditation exist. One of the most popular, known as

Transcendental Meditation (TM), is practiced regularly by more than a million people worldwide. When you do TM, you repeat a carefully chosen word or phrase, called a *mantra*, to focus and calm your mind. Insight Meditation supposedly began 2,500 years ago when the Buddha achieved enlightenment; it's now employed not only by Buddhists, but also by many Westerners. It is taught in medical facilities, including the Stress Reduction Clinic at the University of Massachusetts Medical Center, to aid people with all sorts of health issues. When you practice Insight Meditation, you focus on your breathing and attempt to empty your mind of all thoughts.

You don't even have to sit quietly to meditate—you can take a walk in nature, rake leaves, do yoga, sing, or play a drum, if you like. The point is to put your mind and emotions at ease, and to be in the moment. Anyone can meditate. When looking for the right type of meditation for you, consider finding a teacher, attending a class, or listening to CDs. Experiment with different types of meditation. Determine which approaches feel best for you at this stage of your life's journey. Surrender control. Let your body and its senses talk to you—in other words, go with your intuition. Your body and your intuitive mind will guide you toward the type(s) of meditation best for you.

Here are a few types of meditations you can try, in addition to the breathing meditation given earlier. See which ones suit you best.

Chakra Color Meditation

Eastern medicine associates the colors of the rainbow with seven major energy centers in the body, known as the *chakras* (pronounced SHAH-kras). These chakras align roughly from the base of the spine to the top of the head, and they influence physical and emotional health. By imagining the colors of the visible spectrum shining on these areas of your body during meditation, you can help to keep them functioning optimally.

CHAKRA MEDITATION

Sit or lie in a comfortable place where you won't be disturbed for at least ten to fifteen minutes. Close your eyes.

1. Imagine a ball of red light glowing at the base of your spine.
2. After a minute or two, shift your attention slightly and envision a ball of orange light radiating in the middle of your abdomen.
3. Next, see in your mind's eye a ball of yellow light shining at your solar plexus, about halfway between your belly button and your heart.
4. Then, visualize a ball of green light radiating at your heart center.
5. After a minute or two, imagine a ball of blue light glowing at the base of your throat, between your collarbones.
6. Move your attention to your "third eye," between your eyebrows, and visualize a ball of indigo light shining there.
7. Finally, bring your attention to the top of your head for a minute or so and envision purple light radiating there.
8. When you've finished, slowly open your eyes, feeling refreshed and relaxed.

Silent Meditation

Many meditations are performed silently, while you are sitting still in a quiet place. But you can also engage in silent meditation when you're doing something active, such as taking a walk. Simply set aside your ordinary thoughts—stop thinking about your work, relationships, and other matters—and turn your attention to the present. Silence, in this sense, means being quiet outwardly *and* inwardly.

Sound Meditation

Some people find using sound helps them meditate. TM practitioners use a sound, word, or phrase that has special meaning for them, called a *mantra*, to help induce a state of stillness. You repeat this sound and let it vibrate through your body. Some types of meditation use chanting to shift brainwave frequencies to a meditative level. Other types of sound meditation involve singing, drumming, or playing singing bowls to produce altered states of awareness. Listening to music can also enhance relaxation and mental focus. Choose soothing music that doesn't have a catchy beat or lyrics. You'll find lots of CDs designed to facilitate meditation. Sit quietly, close your eyes, and turn your attention to the music, while you release all distraction and just relax for as long as you like.

Visual Meditation

You can also create a visual image to help quiet your mind. Think of a peaceful, soothing scene, such as waves breaking gently on the beach. Sit or lie in a comfortable place, close your eyes, and bring to mind the scene you've chosen. Release all other thoughts and concerns as you watch this movie in your mind's eye. Feel yourself relaxing and growing more serene as each wave rolls up onto the shore. If your thoughts start to stray, simply bring them back to the scenario and refocus your attention. Continue in this manner for as long as you like.

Guided Meditation

In a guided meditation, someone verbally leads you through a series of steps designed to bring you to a deep state of relaxation. These steps often involve a combination of breathing and visualization techniques. In a meditation class or group, a facilitator may serve as the guide, leading you with a soft, soothing voice. Focusing on the speaker's voice and following his/her instructions enables you to put aside other thoughts and distractions. You'll find lots of CDs that offer guided meditations of various lengths. Or you can record your own voice reading a meditation script that you've created or obtained from a book or an online source.

Physically Active Meditation

Perhaps you've heard about monks raking a Zen garden. That's a form of active meditation. So are yoga and Tai Chi. When you stroll peacefully through the woods or along the beach, letting your mind empty itself of everyday thoughts, you're engaging in this type of meditation, too. You can turn any mundane activity— folding the laundry, washing the dishes, weeding the garden— into a meditation by putting your attention entirely on what you're doing. If your mind starts to wander, gently bring it back to the task at hand.

COUNTING MEDITATION

Begin this meditation by counting backward from fifty by twos. Close your eyes and begin breathing slowly and deeply. Inhale and exhale through your nose.

1. With each breath you take, bring up a number in your mind and count down by twos: 50, 48, 46, 44, and so on. This

requires you to pay attention and focuses your mind. When you reach zero, let your breathing come naturally.

2. Continue focusing on your breathing as you count from 1 to 10, over and over again. See each number in your head or think the number as you breathe naturally.

3. Simply focus on the numbers, over and over again. Let your breath come naturally, without any attempt to control or manipulate it. Observe this rhythm with quiet detachment, without examining, analyzing, or extrapolating.

If you're a beginner, do this meditation for ten minutes; otherwise spend fifteen to twenty minutes per session. This approach should help you focus your attention and put you in a relaxed state of mind. Counting gives your mind something to concentrate on, and you'll have a very clear indication whenever your attention wanders. As soon as you become aware that your focus has shifted to other thoughts, images, or sensations, gently but firmly return to focusing on your breathing and counting.

CHAPTER RECAP

Meditation relaxes and balances your body, mind, and spirit. Meditation trains your mind to become still, rather than restlessly jumping about from thought to thought. Meditation opens your communication channel to the often underused and neglected intuitive side of the brain.

Once a day, starting with ten minutes at a time, sit quietly and practice your meditation and breath work. Build this to twice a day for twenty minutes. Take mini-breaks throughout the day, and pay attention to your breathing. You can do this while sitting at your desk, standing at the kitchen sink, or driving in your car. Commit to meditating daily.

CHAPTER 2

With Eyes Wide Open:
Awesome Auras

"Let the waters settle, you will see the stars and moon mirrored in your being."

—Rumi

An aura is a unique form of energy emanating from you. Your loves, hates, and fears, your pain and pleasures are all reflected in your aura. It's often seen as a colored outline around the head and upper body, creating a halo effect. It can look like a misty white cloud fused with a rainbow or specks of color. Your aura varies in color and size; it can and often does change daily. This energy field alters with your mental and emotional state.

Everyone's aura, or energy field, has its own special intensity of resonance. No one can take this aura from you; it will exist for as long as you live. However, feelings, events, and even people can affect its strength, color, and general appearance.

Psychics and other sensitive individuals can see and/or sense people's auras. By reading this energy, they intuit what's going on with someone emotionally, physically, and otherwise.

Auras have always been an integral part of us. Artwork in many parts of the world has portrayed the aura in religious and cultural paintings and artifacts, from crude paintings on ancient cave walls to Renaissance masterpieces. Such works generally show the aura as a white or gold glow or halo emanating from the heads of saints and religious leaders.

There's an aura around you right now. This doesn't mean you're a saint or guru, but it tells a lot about you and how you relate to the world around you, your personality, your potential, and yes, even what's happening in your life. If only you could read this unique psychic light around the people you know, you could gain insight into them and understand them better.

The good news is, you can. With a little practice you'll be able see, feel, and mentally perceive the auras that surround people. When you master the ability to see auras, you'll notice how thoughts and emotions cause changes in people's personal energy fields. Auras also emanate from plants and animals.

As I discussed before, your thoughts affect your reality and what you experience in life. Your thoughts generate energy, which is reflected in your aura. By observing changes in someone's aura, you can become aware of how that person thinks and feels. You can sense what he or she is likely to be experiencing now and what's likely to transpire in the future as a result of his/her current thoughts.

Perceiving Colors

Without color, our lives would be bleak indeed. Colors brighten our homes, our clothes, our cars, our gardens, and every facet of our lives. Although we may not be conscious of it, colors affect us psychologically, too. Research published in the *New York Times* in February 2009 showed that athletes who wore red were more likely to defeat those who wore blue; that people tended to linger longer in blue rooms than red ones; and that subjects whose test covers were green scored better on IQ tests than people whose covers were red. Each color has psychological and emotional associations. We usually connect red with heat, vitality, action, and passion. Blue, conversely, signifies coolness, tranquility, and relaxation. The colors a psychic sees in a person's aura tell her a lot about that individual's health, temperament, what he's feeling right now, and so on.

SENDING AND RECEIVING COLORS EXERCISE

Because colors have such an obvious impact on us psychologically, you can use them to train your psychic skills. Collect four brightly colored sheets of paper: red, green, blue, and yellow. Invite a few friends or family members to participate in this exercise.

1. Divide the group into "senders" and "receivers" and pair one sender with one receiver. The sender's job is to mentally project an impression of color to the receiver. The receiver's job is to try to intuit which color the sender is thinking about.

2. If you're a receiver, close your eyes and relax. Take several slow, deep breaths, focusing on your inhalations and exhalations in order to calm your mind and get into a receptive psychic mode. As you breathe calmly and slowly, you could say to yourself, "I will be seeing, feeling, or sensing color. I will recognize the color easily."

    If you're a sender, relax by breathing slowly and deeply, focusing on your breath as you prepare your mind. You could say something to yourself like, "I'm going to clearly transfer the color I see" or "I will project the color clearly to the receiver."

3. When everyone is ready, the sender looks at one piece of colored paper and concentrates on it for a few moments, attempting to convey the color mentally to the receiver— without letting the receiver see the paper. The receiver tries to sense the color the sender is transmitting, and writes down her impressions. These impressions may come as a visual image, a sensation, an emotion, or something else. For instance, you may feel heat rather than actually seeing red.

4. The receivers write down what colors they pick up from the senders. Repeat this with each sheet of colored paper. Afterward, compare notes. How well did you do?

5. Switch positions, so now the senders are receivers and vice versa. Try the exercise again. What results did you get this time? Some folks are better at sending, others at receiving. Next, change partners and repeat the exercise. You may discover you can psychically communicate better with one person than another.

The Meaning of Colors

Different cultures assign different meanings to colors. In the West, for example, brides traditionally wear white, but in China they wear red, a color the Chinese consider fortunate. We see color symbolism depicted in spiritual areas, too. The Lakotas, for example, associate colors with the Medicine Wheel, a sacred circle often constructed on the ground and used for healing, teaching, and other purposes. They connect the western part of the circle with black and the unknown, red with the north and wisdom, yellow with the east and new beginnings, and white with the south, the place of healing and regeneration. Blue and green also have spiritual dimensions, because these colors represent the sky and the earth respectively. Christian artists frequently portray Christ and the Virgin Mary dressed in blue, a color associated with compassion and peace. To Hindus, orange (or saffron) is a sacred color that represents purity. Buddhist monks, too, wear saffron-colored robes to signify asceticism and renunciation of the physical world.

Not only do different cultures ascribe different meaning to colors, each of us individually has certain likes and dislikes when it comes to colors. For instance, one person may link pink with love and affection, whereas another considers it a frivolous or "girly" color.

Color Symbolism

The following list provides some information about colors in Western society. But remember, color associations are subjective. What is more important is your personal interpretation of the colors.

Red

We often connect red with aggression and anger ("seeing red") as well as with passion. Red was a favorite of the Romans, and is considered lucky in China and in the practice of feng shui. Casinos use red in their interior design because it makes people forget the time.

Orange

Orange is considered friendly and playful, but also immature—the color of children's toys. Fast food restaurants use orange in their décor because it stimulates the appetite and denotes thriftiness.

Yellow

The color of the sun, yellow enjoys a reputation for conveying cheer and energy. It's also associated with creativity. Vincent van Gogh was particularly fond of yellow, the color of both sunflowers and his home in Arles, France. People tend to connect yellow with caution and temporary things—warning signs and taxis are often yellow, but never banks. Yellow also makes heavy objects seem lighter, and small rooms appear bigger.

Green

We associate green with grass, trees, and nature in general. Thus, it helps to relax us and makes us feel connected to the earth. Because healthy, living plants are green, we link this color with health and nourishment—notice how medical personnel often wear green garb.

Blue

Blue has diverse and often conflicting meanings. Dark shades suggest seriousness and dependability (hence the navy-blue business suit). We link blue with sincerity and call someone who's honest and loyal "true blue." Yet blue also connotes indecency, as in "blue movies," and sadness, as in "the blues." Because blue has a calming effect on us, bridges have been painted blue to deter suicides. A cool, relaxing color, blue makes us think of the sky and gives the feeling of space.

Purple

In ancient cultures, purple was the color of royalty. Today, we still link it with power and prestige, especially of a spiritual nature. Many Western churches use purple in their sanctuary décor and officials' clothing. In Eastern medicine and spirituality, purple is the color of the crown chakra, the body's energy center that connects us to a higher source.

Why Study Colors?

Have fun with the games and exercises provided in this book as you practice stimulating your intuitive mind. Color is very easy to perceive and you may learn to see or sense colors in auras as you train yourself to see more intuitively.

I believe the majority of people see auras, but do not realize it. For instance, how often has your best friend had on a blouse and you think, "Why does she wear that color, it looks horrible on her?" Or, conversely, "That dress makes her look so beautiful." It's possible that the color of the blouse clashed with her aura. The color of the dress that made her look so beautiful may have harmonized with her aura. In both cases, you read your friend's aura. Maybe you've worn a color one day and received lots of compliments, but a few weeks later when you wore the same color no one said a thing. It is quite possible your state of mind or emotions changed during that time, and so did your aura.

You can use the color descriptions given above as a starting point for interpreting the moods, attitudes, and health of the people you meet—but don't let these meanings limit you. Always go with your own feelings and impressions.

Kirlian Photography

Some parapsychologists claim auras are biophysical energy emissions, and believe Kirlian photography captures auras on film. Named for Semyon Kirlian, a Russian inventor who discovered the technique in 1939, it supposedly depicts the energy field that surrounds not only humans, but animals, plants, and even inanimate objects.

Other experimenters say there is no evidence that Kirlian photography depicts the human aura or energy field. It's also been suggested that because the colors emerge on Polaroid film according to the length of development time, the process may be manipulated to show whatever the photographer wants to show. The technique has been studied extensively for many years, yet debate continues about Kirlian photography's validity.

How Kirlian Photography Works

On the International Parapsychology Research Foundation's website, Brian Schill, a paranormal investigator, explains, "During the photographic procedure, an object or body part, such as a person's hand, is placed on photographic paper or film in an apparatus that generates a high-voltage, low-amperage, high-frequency electric current. The resulting photo shows an electrical discharge or 'halo' that surrounds the outline of the object."

How Kirlian Photography Can Help

According to the some researchers and healers who use Kirlian photography, the technique shows the energy flow in a subject's body. Additionally, it reveals how thoughts, emotions, stress, illness, and other things such as the foods a person eats affect her aura—it may even help detect the early stages of a disease. "Before and after" photos enable a practitioner to see changes in the patient's energy and to monitor these changes over time.

From the perspective of psychic development, it can be useful to compare a Kirlian photograph with what you see intuitively. Is the image on the photo similar to what you noticed? If not, don't despair. Remember, even in the physical world not all people see colors the same way. Trust your instincts as you continue developing this aspect of your "second sight."

How Negative Energy Affects Your Aura

Negative thoughts and feelings are fiercely powerful. Thoughts *are* energy. As I discussed earlier, the mind is a formidable resource that creates your future reality through the energy of thought. If, for example, your thoughts are filled with doom and gloom, hatred, jealousy, fear, or passion for revenge, you'll attract the consequences of those thoughts into your life. On the other hand, if you cultivate thoughts of love, understanding, and forgiveness, you're more likely to receive positive things in return.

Positive thinking can even extend your life, according to a study of more than a thousand people over the age of fifty published in the *American Chronicle* in October 2006. The study found that on average, people with positive attitudes lived nearly eight years longer than their pessimistic peers.

As I've already mentioned, the energy generated by thoughts and emotions imprints the aura. Psychics read this energy and may see it as colors in someone's aura. For instance, if you see red in someone's aura you might sense that person's temper, passion, or sexuality. Again, your interpretation and the feelings you pick up when you see or sense a specific color are what count.

When Your Aura Is Low

Mental, emotional, and physical conditions all affect your aura. A "low" aura—one that appears dull or faint, contains dark or murky colors, or doesn't extend very far from your body—indicates low vitality and could mean you have a mental, emotional, or physical problem. Depression, for example, weakens the energy of your aura. So do stress and anxiety. If you feel these emotions might be draining your vitality, you can improve your mental health with meditation, diet, and exercise.

Sensing Violent Energy

Fear changes your aura, too. Crimes of violence and hate leave intense energy in their wake that a psychic can sense. Because energy cannot be destroyed, it remains in the environment after an act of violence has occurred, and leaves energy clues a psychic detective can follow. A crime of passion or hate can be readily deciphered psychically. Missing persons cases may not involve acts of intense emotion; therefore, they are harder for me to sense psychically. In a case of homicide that has left violent psychic energy behind, I can confidently communicate my impressions to law enforcement authorities who have reached an investigative dead end.

When I collaborate with police on a homicide case, I request that they send me something that was on the victim's body at the time of his death. It could be a ring, watch, belt, shoe, or a lock of hair. The victim's intense thoughts and emotions just before death infused his aura with energy, leaving traces on anything that touched his body. The energy of this horrific event has been left behind and can be interpreted psychically.

With such energy-imprinted item(s), I can proceed with my job. I prefer to work in a quiet environment, devoid of as many distractions as possible. I clear my own mental clutter, and then open myself up to the sensations—visuals, sounds, smells, feelings—that come into my mind's eye. I allow myself to witness the emotions, sensations, and events that happened to and around the homicide victim.

Thankfully, most of us won't have to experience the violent energies connected with murder. But you will likely come into contact with some form of negative energy in your environment. Negative energy has many sources, including the people around you, so it's important to learn how to shield yourself from "bad vibes" that can adversely impact your own energy field.

Energy Vampires

Yep, they exist. Normal-looking folks who drain your energy without realizing it. Maybe you know people who do nothing but complain and gripe, or who put a negative spin on everything. They are usually very bitter, angry, or self-centered individuals and their problems, their needs, are their only focus. You may notice you become fatigued after spending a short time with these folks. They "bum you out," so to speak. Their negativity brings you down and depletes your energy. They sap your vitality, and a psychic can see this change reflected in your aura.

How to Protect Yourself

Obviously, allowing other people to devitalize you isn't a good thing emotionally, physically, or psychically. I don't mean you shouldn't be patient and considerate toward a friend who's having a bad day, or not lend someone a shoulder to cry on. But energy vampires *never* seem to have a good day, and they air their complaints constantly to anyone who'll listen. You can take steps to counteract the effects of an energy vampire.

1. Once you recognize these folks, you can put a mental protective barrier around yourself to shield you from their negativity. Mentally imagine a white light surrounding you like a bubble that prevents any negative energy from entering into your auric field. You can also do this visualization as a general preventive measure every time you meditate.

2. Another way is to say to yourself when you greet the energy vampire, "The love in me greets the love in you," or "The good person in me greets the good person in you." Spiritual teachers tell us that underneath even the most unpleasant person's exterior lies inner goodness, the "divine within." It's amazing how sometimes just realizing this can neutralize a negative environment or encounter.

3. You can also project positive energy through your aura by focusing on positive thoughts. Prayer, too, is a strong tool that invites higher forces (guides, angels, your higher self) to assist you. At the same time, build a protective shield around yourself as described above.

4. Keep your visits with vampires short. While they are complaining, think positive thoughts and try not to get emotionally involved with their problems. Instead of reacting defensively, try to remain detached. If possible, redirect the conversation to more positive topics. Or point out as tact-

fully as you can that you'd rather not focus on unpleasant subjects.

5. Cross your arms as casually as you can over your solar plexus, which is located about halfway between your belly button and the base of your sternum. Eastern medicine refers to this area as the solar plexus chakra, and considers it to be the locus of self-confidence. Your crossed arms physically shield this chakra and your self-esteem from being adversely affected by the vampire's negative energy.

SUSAN'S STORY

Susan, a physically beautiful woman, was a student and friend of mine. She went through a nasty divorce. Anger, bitterness, and hatred toward her husband consumed her. Susan's strong negative emotions created a minor illness within her body. She visited my house and asked me to energize her with my hands so that she would feel better. I stood behind her chair with my eyes closed and placed my hands around her head where normally her aura could be felt. But I felt nothing. I kept inadvertently bumping her head with my hands. I thought it was strange, but I didn't actually tune in to why her aura was so low, mainly because she'd asked me to help her to heal and that was my focus. I concluded that her illness and devastating divorce had depleted her aura. (Later, I'll talk more about the importance of asking the right questions when you seek advice from a psychic, in order to get the answers you really need. Had Susan asked me why her aura was so low, I might have been able to see what lay around the corner.)

A few days later, Susan almost died in a terrible automobile accident. Her beautiful face was mangled. In many places, her slender body was broken. I believe her negative thinking brought on the accident, unconsciously of course—no one would knowingly seek such trauma. However, her young son, who was with her in the car, escaped without a scratch.

I began working with Susan in the hospital, as she went through grueling treatments and anxious hours. I was able to convince her of the power, energy, and potential for healing that her own thoughts held. While medical science and physicians labored through surgical procedures and treatments to put her face and body back together, she meditated daily. In her meditations and visualization exercises, she projected images and thoughts of love and healing. She listened to healing tapes, both subliminal and positive thinking. Her steady recovery after each operation amazed many.

After her divorce, with terrible scars still visible on her face and yet more surgery needed, she grew determined to fall in love again. I suggested that she learn to project beauty and love and hope, by thinking of herself as loving and beautiful and by sending out loving, hopeful thoughts to others. She put this suggestion into practice through meditation. So I wasn't surprised when she met and married a handsome younger man. How I wish I had been present at their first encounter to witness firsthand the lovely shades of their auras. I know the sight must have been glorious!

What Happens to Your Aura When You Die?

While you're alive, your aura emits energetic messages that sensitive individuals can read. It recedes during a physical or mental illness, sometimes turning a weak gray, and then vanishes just before death. Your aura dissipates and separates from your physical body when you die. Because your aura is made of energy, and energy can't be destroyed, your aura isn't destroyed. But no one really knows where that energy goes. Some suggest it merges with the collective energy in the universe; others think it may regroup when you reincarnate.

In his booklet *Auras*, avid aura reader Edgar Cayce described an experience that impressed me. While visiting on one of the floors of a large department store, he pushed the button for the elevator. When the elevator door opened, he saw that it was crowded with holiday shoppers, but there was enough room for him to squeeze in. Nevertheless, he decided not to enter. The door closed and the elevator plummeted and crashed. Everyone inside the elevator was killed. He realized later that he had not seen any auras around the occupants of the ill-fated elevator. Cayce had responded to an intuitive feeling relayed by the intuitive side of his brain.

Learning to See Auras

We live in a universe comprised of energy. Everything, animate and inanimate, is composed of and radiates energy. Auras reveal the energy that emanates from us and collects around us. The energy in living things changes; nonliving energy doesn't. Energy moves through each of us at a different rate, rhythm, or pattern. Everything and everyone has a unique vibration, which psychics can sense. A person's energetic vibration is like a fingerprint; no two are alike.

READING THE ENERGY OF AN ANIMATE OBJECT

See what your friend's aura looks like.

1. Have your friend stand in front of the light-colored wall.
2. Stare at your friend's "third eye," the area slightly above the bridge of the nose, between the two biological eyes. According to Eastern medicine, this is one of the body's main energy centers, known as the brow chakra, and the locus of intuition. You'll soon see a glow of energy around the head and upper body. That's your friend's aura. Keep focusing on your friend's third eye as you count to six.
3. Ask the person to move aside quickly. Look at where he was standing. Do you see light around the area where your friend's head and shoulders were? Do you see a glow on the wall after he moved? The afterimage you see contains energy left from your friend's energy field or aura. Now repeat the experiment, making notes each time.

The more you practice this technique, the sooner you'll see color. White light contains all the colors of the spectrum and is easier to see—but you'll notice other colors as you become accustomed to using your vision with greater awareness. One color might be more prominent, but you'll probably notice several. Seeing auras lets you know instantly what's going on emotionally and physically with the people you encounter. It's an important step toward expanding your psychic ability.

READING THE ENERGY OF AN
INANIMATE OBJECT

Meditate for a few minutes to prepare yourself before you do this exercise. Seek the assistance of a friend or family member.

1. Collect several pieces of red, green, blue, or yellow paper. Draw a dark circle in the middle of each piece of paper.

2. Your helper should stand in front of a light-colored wall (or hang a white sheet by taping it to a wall) while you sit or stand six to ten feet away. Ask your helper to extend her arm outward, holding a piece of colored paper.

3. Stare for a minute at the paper, focusing your eyes on the circle you drew. Try not to blink. Keep staring at the circle. As you do this, you should notice in your peripheral vision a light glow or halo effect around the circle and the paper itself.

4. Keep your eyes focused on the circle. Count to four and have your friend quickly remove the paper while you continue to look at the paper's former location. A glow of light or what we call an afterimage should appear on the wall. This afterimage contains energy left behind by the object, the energy of its aura. Notice how long the image stays. Does it move? What color did you see? Record what you've seen this first time.

5. Try it again. Experiment with paper of different colors, marked with dark circles to give you a focal point. Again, make notes about what you experience.

SEEING COMBINED AURAS

This exercise continues honing your perception and lets you see how other people interact at an energetic level. You'll need two people to help with this exercise.

1. Have one of the helpers stand in front of the wall. Concentrate on seeing that person's aura.
2. Once you've seen it, ask the second person to slowly move toward the first participant. Become aware of the second person's aura.
3. What happens when the auras of these two people meet? With practice, you should be able to see how one person's aura affects the other's. Some auras converge, others diverge. A private, skeptical, or cautious person will put up an energetic shield that deflects the other person's aura. A trusting, loving, or open-minded person's aura will be receptive to the other individual's energy and join with it. The auras of two people who distrust or dislike each other would, of course, diverge. Two lovers' auras would converge. It's fascinating to see.

What If You Don't See Anything?

If nothing happens when you try to see an aura, don't be concerned. Most folks don't see auras, at least not until they've honed their perception skills. I can only see an aura if the person is standing in front of a light background. You may pick up this energy mentally and get feelings, or "vibes," from other people. Just as your physical sense of smell or hearing may be stronger than your ordinary visual ability, you may be able to sense things intuitively through means other than vision. That's okay. Go with your strengths.

FEELING AURAS

Even if you can't see auras, you may be able to feel them. Try this exercise with a friend or family member. Before you begin, both of you should relax and do a few breathing exercises to center yourselves.

1. Ask your friend or family member to sit, while you stand behind him with your eyes closed. Tell yourself that you *will* be able to sense this person's aura.

2. Place your hands on either side of his head, palms facing in, about four to six inches away from actually touching his head.

3. What sensations do you pick up? Do you feel warmth? Coolness? Lightness or heaviness? Something else? Do you associate these sensations with a particular color? For instance, you might connect warmth with red or orange.

4. Drop your hands and step away from the person. Discuss your perceptions with your subject to better understand what you felt in his aura and how it relates to what he's experiencing.

Everyone can develop his or her own style of perceiving auras. Sensing energy—seeing it visually, feeling it, or picking it up mentally—is how psychics understand things other people don't.

Time and distance aren't obstacles, either. Psychics can sense and interpret energy over the phone, through walls, or across oceans. And, as I explained earlier, we can even pick up vibes from the past, as I do when I'm assisting police in solving crimes, because energy can never be destroyed.

COLOR SENSING EXERCISE

This exercise can help you sense colors and fine-tune your perceptual ability. Each color of the spectrum has a different wavelength, and you may be able to intuitively discern their different resonances.

1. Don't watch as a friend places four green sheets of paper into four opaque envelopes, then puts one red sheet of paper into a fifth identical envelope.
2. When she's finished, hold each envelope, one at a time, in your hand. See if you can sense which one contains the red paper.

EXERCISE YOUR VISUALIZATION MUSCLES

This meditation exercises your "visualization muscles" and helps you strengthen your imagination. You might ask someone to read the following list to you as you enter into meditation. Alternatively, you could record yourself reading it, and then listen to it as you meditate.

1. Take a deep breath, inhaling through your nose to the count of four. Hold your breath to a count of seven. Exhale slowly through your mouth to a count of eight.
2. In your imagination, look down at your feet. Imagine they are on a path. Take three or four steps on this path and enter a field of red flowers. The red flowers surround you and give you energy. Stop and imagine lying down on the earth, surrounded by the red flowers.
3. Breathe in deeply again through your nose for a count of four, hold for a count of seven, exhale through your mouth

for a count of eight. As you breathe in this manner, concentrate on your breath and on the color red.

4. As you continue breathing this way, imagine the red energy
    flowing into your body with each inhalation. You can feel
    the red energy as it flows through your body, enhancing the
    energy of all your organs.

5. Thank the earth for supporting and nourishing you. Thank
    the earth for providing you with energy. Breathe normally.

6. Now, in your imagination, stand up and mentally take a few
    more steps. You will come to a lake and see the orange sun
    above it. The brilliant orange orb of the sun is reflected in
    the still water.

7. Stop and breathe in the color orange. Take a deep breath
    for a count of four, hold for a count of seven, exhale for
    a count of eight. Imagine you're breathing in the orange
    color that is reflected in the water; experience how this
    energy saturates your body. Feel how it illuminates you.

8. Concentrate on your breath and the color orange. Your body
    absorbs the energy and sensation of orange. Feel how this
    color stimulates you. Let yourself become invigorated and
    transformed by the orange color. Sense the powers of the
    water. Look into the water for a long time. Breathe normally
    for a few moments.

9. Continue your journey as the sun slowly rises and
    changes into a radiant yellow. In your imagination, walk
    toward a field of bright yellow flowers. Sit or lie down in
    the field and absorb this yellow color. Take a deep breath
    as you count to four, hold for a count of seven, exhale for
    a count of eight.

10. Feel an opening, expansive sensation in your solar plexus
    as you mentally enjoy the sight of the yellow flowers. The

yellow energy warms your body and makes you feel joyful as you relax and open yourself to the yellow light of the sun and the flowers.

11. The path now leads you to a hill. Sense yourself walking through a green meadow to the edge of the forest. Stop under the green canopy of a large tree. The hanging branches, with their delicate green leaves, surround you like a tent.

12. Breathe. Don't worry about counting now, just breathe naturally. The wind whispers quietly through the leaves. Let it gently blow through you as well. Feel your heart opening wide and absorbing the color green, which is soothing and healing.

13. Your path now takes you a few steps up a mountain. The blue sky arches above you. Let yourself be enveloped and illuminated by the blue of the heavens. In this heavenly blue, you encounter a sense of peace that penetrates your earthly existence in a healing way. Breathe in the calming energy of the blue light.

14. Continue to walk. See yourself standing in front of a chapel. You enter it and stop in the anteroom. Indigo-blue panes of glass give the room an atmosphere of peace. Breathe in this indigo-colored light. The deep blue color calms your mind and awakens an awareness of the divine world within you. Let yourself merge with the energy of this color. Breathe naturally.

15. Go deeper inside the chapel. The sun now shines through violet windowpanes. You notice a wonderful violet amethyst on the altar. Light shines through the gemstone, flooding you with violet light. Inhale the color. Feel how the violet penetrates your entire being. You would like to stay here.

Everything around you is very quiet and everything within you is silent. You have arrived. You sense that you are where you belong.

16. Breathe, focusing on the color you think you need most. Red brings vitality; orange is invigorating; yellow is uplifting; green offers healing; blue calms you; indigo heightens your awareness; violet connects you to the spiritual realm. Imagine this color shining all around you, nourishing you. Enjoy it balancing and harmonizing your mind and body, giving you whatever you need to feel whole.

17. Stay in this serene place for as long as you want. When you're ready to leave this wonderful inner reality, move your fingers a little as you breathe deeply and slowly. Gradually, open your eyes.

CHAPTER RECAP

Just as each of us is physically unique, each of us has an aura like no one else's. Furthermore, our auras can change from day to day as our moods and emotions change. Outside events that trigger your emotions can affect your aura and the energy emanating from your being. Negative emotions are just as potent as positive ones; perhaps more so.

Sometimes you sense vibes coming from others without realizing you are picking up the energy of their auras. Negative people can deplete your vitality. However, by learning to read other people's auras and focusing your own energy, you not only protect yourself from being influenced by unwanted energies in your environment, you strengthen your ability to perceive beyond the mundane, material world.

CHAPTER 3

Listening to Your Intuition

"It is our duty as men and women to proceed as though the limits of our abilities do not exist."

—Pierre Teilhard de Chardin

Your mind is a wonderful tool, a resource you can apply in any way you wish. You can opt to use as much or as little of it as you want. You can limit or expand your consciousness. Developing your psychic potential enables you to use more of your brainpower than most people ordinarily do.

I share the view held by many that every outer effect is the natural expression of an inner thought pattern. If you subscribe to this view, it is a waste of time and energy to try to struggle with situations, people, or events in the outer world in order to change them. You'll have more success if you concentrate on changing your own thought patterns. Your current thoughts are something you *can* control, and by doing so, you exercise more control over your present circumstances as well as your future.

Change Your Thinking, Change Your Life

In other words, you create your own life experiences, your own happiness and unhappiness, with your thought patterns.

That's a pretty powerful concept, and one that might seem surprising or unrealistic to you. But think for a moment about a time when you were having a bad day. From the minute you crawled out of bed, everything seemed to go wrong. The more irritable and impatient you got, the more obstacles popped up to further frustrate you. Now remember a time when the opposite happened and things flowed smoothly. Everything seemed to go right—each traffic light you came to was green, no one was ahead of you in the supermarket line, you got a bargain at your favorite store, and so on. Maybe there was a connection between your attitude and your experiences.

You've heard the old saying about seeing the glass as either half-full or half-empty. It's true that your perceptions and expectations are responsible for how you interpret your life. Sometimes things that seem unfortunate at first glance turn out to be beneficial in the long run. For instance, you might have to wait longer than you'd expected in the dentist's reception room, but while you're waiting you have time to read an interesting magazine article you might have missed otherwise. It's always your choice how you wish to view a situation and how you deal with circumstances that may not have been part of your conscious plan.

CROSS OUT NEGATIVE THOUGHTS

You really can change your life by changing your perceptions. Here's a simple and effective exercise you can do to shift your reality.

Start paying attention to your thoughts. The next time a negative one pops into your mind, envision the thought surrounded by one of those red circles with a diagonal line through it that means "No." Then replace the thought with something positive. Maybe someone cuts in front of you while you're driving and grabs the parking space you'd targeted for yourself. Your first reaction might be an angry thought (or even a few choice words) directed at the other driver. Instead, quickly cross out the angry thought and bless the person instead. Then drive on, confident that you'll find another parking space.

Notice what happens when you shift your mental gears this way. You don't carry the initial tension with you and let it interfere with the rest of your day. You might even find a better parking space.

If you continue doing this exercise regularly, you'll soon realize you've effectively reduced the stress in your life. Little things that once upset you don't matter so much anymore. You've become more accepting and less judgmental of other people and yourself. Your relationships have improved. Your path has become smoother. You've changed your life.

Stress, anger, and anxiety interfere with your ability to receive information from your intuitive mind. When you let yourself get upset, it's hard to hear the voice within that is always trying to guide you. That's one reason why I encourage meditation as a way to quiet your mind and emotions. When your conscious, rational mind is calm and centered, you can pick up the signals your intuition sends you.

MEDITATION TO LINK LOGIC AND INTUITION

This meditation uses both the logical, verbal part of your mind and the intuitive, visual part. By strengthening both parts of your mind and the connection between them, you can tap more of your personal power and enhance your ability to function on every level—psychically and rationally.

1. Before you begin, select a subject for your meditation. It should be something you can conceive of visually as well as verbally—an object, animal, place. You might choose something you'd like to gain insight into, although that's not essential for this meditation to produce benefits. (Don't choose a person, however.)

2. Sit in a place where you feel comfortable, and where you won't be disturbed for at least ten minutes.

3. Close your eyes and relax, using deep breathing exercises or whatever method you prefer.

4. When you feel calm and ready, bring to mind the word that expresses what you've opted to contemplate in this meditation: house, tree, lake, dog, tulip, chair, jacket, apple, or whatever you've chosen. Visualize the word itself, spelled out.

5. Hold the word in your mind for as long as you can.

6. When the letters begin to fade or your mind begins to wander, change to envisioning a picture of that object. See it as clearly as you can. Pay attention to details—shutters on the house, leaves on the tree, spots on the dog's fur.

7. After a while, shift back to seeing the word in your mind's eye and hold this as long as possible.

8. Go back to picturing the object.

9. Continue shifting back and forth for ten minutes or so. Allow your mind to keep exploring the subject of your meditation in greater detail or expanding your observation of it more broadly.

10. Notice any feelings, insights, or impressions that arise during this process.

11. When you are ready, slowly bring your attention back to the present and open your eyes.

12. Record your experience in a journal, including any emotions, ideas, sensations, and/or information you received while meditating.

What Is Your Intuition Trying to Tell You?

Albert Einstein, one of the great geniuses of our time, wrote in *Cosmic Religion*, "I believe in intuition and inspiration. Imagination is more important than knowledge." Your intuitive mind is constantly working for you, although you may not realize it. How often have you heard someone say he made a decision by listening to his heart? Of course, we know the heart does not speak. What people really mean is they are listening to their intuition.

If you listen to your intuition, it will provide the answers you need to make the right decisions. In 2007, Carlin Flora reported in *Psychology Today* the results of a study done by a group of researchers at the University of London. They "found that people who went with their initial response on a test of visual perception . . . did better than those who were given more time to ponder."

PAY ATTENTION TO HUNCHES

We've all had the experience of ignoring a gut feeling and wishing later that we'd followed the hunch. Our intuition knows what's best for us, but often we second-guess ourselves and choose to go with logic instead.

The next time you get a hunch, notice how fast your rational mind jumps in to argue the point. For example, you might have had a feeling you should take a different route than the one MapQuest suggested, but ultimately decided to follow the map's instructions anyway—and ended up stuck in a road construction delay. Even though your intuitive impressions may seem illogical, practice following them. Don't let logic convince you otherwise. See what happens if you feel drawn into a store you'd never consider entering ordinarily; you might find something you've been looking for or run into an old acquaintance you haven't seen in a long time. By paying more attention to your intuition, you'll strengthen your connection with it and increase the benefits you derive from its wisdom.

THE DANGER OF IGNORING INTUITION

Even though my intuitive mind sends me messages regularly, I occasionally have ignored them—usually to my peril. One day as I waited in my doctor's office to get a prescription filled, his nurse practitioner approached me. I immediately picked up on her negative energy and felt a sense of danger, which seemed an odd thing to feel in a doctor's office. I followed her into the examining room, where she wanted to give me a physical. I told her I had only come to get my prescription refilled, but she handed me a paper cup and told me to give her a specimen. The negative vibes and sense of danger grew stronger, and I kept thinking, *I have to get out of here.*

Even though I insisted I didn't need a physical, the nurse practitioner seemed bent on giving me one anyway. The angry energy I felt emanating from her continued to escalate. Against my intuition's better judgment, I agreed to let her take my vital signs. She weighed me and measured my height (incorrectly). Then without checking my blood pressure—usually one of the first things a nurse does—she grabbed my arm and jabbed a needle in my vein to draw blood. I told her to be careful, but she continued plunging the needle into my arm again and again, until I almost screamed in pain and blood spilled down my arm. Finally, I extricated myself from her and left the office, with blood still dripping from my arm.

Because my initial, gut reaction hadn't seemed logical, I'd allowed rational thinking to override my intuition. As a result, I suffered needlessly.

Although ignoring your intuition may not result in your getting jabbed with a needle, it could lead to other unhappy consequences, such as taking the wrong job, making an unprofitable investment, getting into an argument, and so on. Your intuitive mind knows what's best for you. If you follow its guidance, it will usually alert you to potential problems and steer you toward the people and situations that will benefit you most.

The Language of Symbols

Why don't we always recognize or understand what the intuition tells us? It's most often because the psychic/intuitive mind speaks in the language of symbols, not in complete, grammatically correct sentences, similar to how dreams communicate valuable information to us through symbols and imagery. But if you can learn to interpret the symbols and images, your intuitive mind will guide, inspire, and assist you in countless ways.

Here's an example. A woman found herself hopelessly lost while driving at night on unfamiliar country roads. Confused, desperate, and panicky, she suddenly saw a delivery truck for the Safeway supermarket chain. The lost woman's intuition symbolically associated the name Safeway with finding a "safe way" out of her predicament. She followed the truck and it led her back to the main route she'd been searching for.

Common Symbols

Here are some common, familiar symbols we find in cultures around the world and the meanings generally attached to them:

- **Circle:** unity, harmony, wholeness
- **Square:** stability, permanence
- **Triangle:** trinity, growth, reaching for greater heights
- **Arrow:** movement, direction
- **Spiral:** life energy
- **Cross:** union of spirit and matter
- **Star:** hope, promise

Recognizing Your Personal Symbols

Each of us has a unique set of personal symbols as well as the greater cultural symbols we use. Let your intuition guide you in interpreting yours. Start keeping a journal of symbols, and describe what they mean to you. Note your experiences related to various symbols and signs. Maybe you'll discover that finding a penny on the street means you'll soon receive a sum of money, or that seeing a rainbow means good luck is coming your way. Understanding your personal symbols can let you catch a glimpse of the future, prepare for upcoming events, give you warnings, and much more.

Intuition and Creative Breakthroughs

Dramatic, creative breakthroughs frequently emerge from intuition. Successful people are much more likely than other folks to use both logic and intuition. Bill Gates, Microsoft's founder, is one of them. His advice is, "Often you have to rely on intuition." Thomas Edison is another who relied on his intuitive ability to guide him—the inspiration that led to the invention of the electric light bulb came to him in a dream.

Thirteen thousand business executives in a study conducted by Harvard researcher Dr. Jagdish Parikh said that 80 percent of their business success came from relying on their intuition. Research done by Ashley Fields, a senior advisor to Shell Oil, supports Parikh's findings and notes that among Fortune 500 companies, "intuitive information processing strategies are most often found at the highest levels of an organization."

MISUNDERSTANDING THE INTUITIVE MIND'S MESSAGES

At times we sense the intuitive mind communicating with us, but still misinterpret its message. Some years ago, I couldn't shake the feeling of death around me. It hung in the air like a heavy fog for weeks. I knew death was close by, and concluded it was my own. I wasn't upset; in fact I felt very calm, which in itself was strange.

I started getting my personal effects in order, including all the files I had kept on the police cases I had worked on during the past last thirty-five years; they were my most valuable assets. I made a new will and wanted my brother, who was several years younger than me, to be the executor. I had not seen him in years, and felt an urgent wish to visit him and explain my upcoming death. On the phone, I didn't tell him why I wanted to visit him and his wife, but said I wanted to see him soon and suggested a time. He was surprised, but open to my visit.

I flew down to his home a few weeks later. We had a most enjoyable time together, talking about the past and the adventures we'd had together when we were younger. Sharing stories and discussing our accomplishments was fun, until I started to talk about my impending death. He didn't want to hear a word about death, but he agreed to be the executor of my will. Four months later my brother died suddenly. It was his death, not mine, that I had picked up on intuitively.

USE YOUR FIVE SENSES TO STRENGTHEN YOUR SIXTH SENSE

You can improve your intuition so it enhances the creative aspects of your professional and personal life.

Ask a friend to place a number of fragrant items before you on a table one by one, such as a piece of just-cooked bacon, a sprig of lavender, a clove of fresh garlic, a piece of new leather, and some mothballs. Close your eyes and smell each one individually. Let your sensory vision translate these scents into mental images. Try to clearly "see" these scents interpreted as pictures in your mind's eye. Practice with a variety of aromatic items. Over time, this exercise helps you connect your sensory/visual abilities and strengthens the creative part of your mind, which is also the seat of intuition.

While in a waking state, we don't always hear or listen to our intuitive warnings, which can sometimes be rather faint. In such instances, our dreams may step in and send the warnings to us while we sleep—and if we don't pay attention, they tend to get louder and more insistent.

A while back I needed an attorney, and a friend recommended someone he knew. I met the attorney, explained my case, and hired him. A few weeks later I started to have verbal fights with him in my dreams. Soon the dreams turned into nightmares—night after night I found myself yelling at the attorney.

Soon it became clear that he was not qualified to work on my case and my best interest wasn't a top priority for him. He made decisions without informing me of his actions. He stalled and delayed filing motions. The yelling moved from the dream state to the waking one. I fired him and found a wonderful attorney. (I'll talk more about dreams and how they speak to us in Chapter 13.)

Using Logic and Intuition Together

Poker offers us an example of how logic and intuition function in collaboration. A poker player uses his logical mind for crucial information about the hand he is holding: its mathematical possibilities. He can calculate his chances by observing what cards have already been turned up, how many cards the other players have taken or discarded, and so forth.

But usually that's not enough, as any gambler will tell you. What does the intuitive side of his mind have to say? Is he mentally picking up emotional signals from the other players? Does his intuition tell him another player is bluffing? "Hold 'em or fold 'em" decisions often require consensus between the logical mind and the intuitive mind. In life, as in poker, we need to use all the resources available to us.

Intuition and Medicine

A good example of rational thinking and intuition functioning together comes from the medical world. The University of Minnesota reports a study done in 2001 of 262 registered nurses concerning their use of intuition in their work. The nurses said they regularly used intuition in the form of "gut feelings" in their interactions with their patients. Another study in 2003 of physicians found "overwhelming agreement that intuition plays a vital role in the practice of family medicine."

Did you know there's even such a thing as a medical intuitive? In 1973, neurosurgeon C. Norman Shealy, MD, PhD, who coined the term, began testing the ability of sensitive individuals to diagnose medical conditions intuitively, without benefit of logical information. His studies showed Caroline Myss to be 93 percent accurate at psychically seeing health problems. Since then, Myss has worked with Dr. Shealy and independently to expand the role of intuition as a diagnostic tool, and she has become a renowned authority in the field.

During the early part of the twentieth century, psychic Edgar Cayce spent forty years diagnosing illnesses and recommending cures for thousands of people. Cayce had no medical training and only an eighth-grade education, yet he could go into a trance and intuitively see what was ailing someone and what would heal the problem. Chapter 8 has more information on using your psychic abilities to deal with medical problems.

Use More of Your Brain

Most of us tend to be more oriented toward either rational thinking or intuitive thinking. But why use only half your brain? You wouldn't use only one arm or one leg, would you? If you rely mostly on logical thinking, you can exercise your intuitive mind by working jigsaw puzzles, writing or drawing with your left hand, or inventing fanciful stories that have little logic to them. If you tend to rely more on your intuition, exercise your logical brain by playing Scrabble, doing crossword puzzles or Sudoku, or writing step-by-step how-to instructions for something you like to do. (Test your success by asking someone to follow those instructions to find out how well you conveyed the instructions.)

It will do little good if you try these exercises only once or twice. Set aside some time each day to work on them. Simply trying will give you new insight into how your brain works.

CHAPTER RECAP

Some of the world's best and brightest thinkers rely on a combination of both logic and intuition. By combining both parts of your brain, you'll get the edge on people who choose to follow only one or the other. One way to strengthen your sixth sense is to improve your awareness of the five ordinary senses.

The intuitive mind speaks to us in the language of symbols and imagery. Some symbols are commonly understood by people in many cultures, but each of us has our own collection of unique, personal symbols as well. Paying attention to your individual symbols and keeping a journal of them can help you interpret what your subconscious mind is trying to tell you. Creative breakthroughs often result from realizing and following your intuitive mind's guidance.

CHAPTER 4

Telepathy: Communicating Without Your iPhone

"Life is measured by the number of things you are alive to."
— Malathie D. Babcock

Telepathy is mind-to-mind communication. You don't need an iPhone, computer, or other device to share your ideas with someone else—you don't even have to speak.

The term comes from the Greek *tele*, meaning distant, and *patheia*, meaning seeing. In 1882, Frederic W. H. Myers, cofounder of the Society for Psychical Research in London, coined the word to refer to a type of ESP.

We've all had the experience of answering a phone call and knowing who was on the other end of the line without checking caller ID. Telepathic communication includes thoughts, ideas, impressions, feelings, sensations, and mental imagery. Some folks hear words, while others get clear visual impressions or see flashes of mental images. Still others experience emotional reactions or physical sensations.

Telepathy offers us a fascinating world to study, learn, and experience firsthand. We can discover much about ourselves, our psychic abilities, and how we communicate with one another by exploring telepathy. We also can have fun.

Here's an example of telepathy. A woman is driving to work when she sees a dead cat on the side of the road. Immediately, she thinks of a coworker and friend so strongly that she consciously wonders, *Why did I think of him when I saw the cat? He doesn't even like cats.* When she gets to work, her friend, very upset, confesses that his car hit a cat on his way to work. It was the very same cat she had seen.

This telepathic experience contains two important factors:

1. The two people are friends and might be said to be on the same wavelength.
2. Strong emotion is present—the man is deeply upset about killing the cat.

The strength of a relationship is important in day-to-day telepathic experiences. In experiments and exercises, however, telepathic sending and receiving can be achieved even among strangers if the sender's concentration is strong and the receiver is open.

Studying Telepathy

Early tests of telepathic abilities, conducted in the late nineteenth century, were pretty rudimentary. A sender was placed in one room and instructed to try to mentally transmit a two-digit number, a taste, or a visual image to a receiver in another room. Results were recorded and researchers made efforts to arrive at some conclusions about telepathy and telepathic communications.

In the early 1930s, J. B. Rhine and his colleagues at Duke University began using a special deck of cards designed by Karl Zener to study ESP. The deck of Zener cards contained twenty-five cards illustrated with simple geometric designs: circles, crosses, wavy lines, squares, and stars. These cards were adopted as the standard means for telepathy testing.

Tests were usually conducted with sender and receiver in the same location. However, distance seems to be no obstacle. In February 1971, astronaut Edgar D. Mitchell mentally sent the Zener symbols to four human receivers while he was near the moon, some 200,000 miles from Earth. Even though he was only moderately successful, the results far exceeded Mitchell's expectations.

EXPERIMENTING WITH ZENER CARDS

For this experiment, you can use the Zener cards as described above, purchased from a bookstore, or you can make your own using index cards. A deck of Zener cards consists of twenty-five unnumbered cards displaying five separate images (circles, crosses, wavy lines, squares, and stars), five of each image. You have a one in five chance that any given card design lies on top of the deck or is being viewed by the sender.

1. The sender first draws a card and looks intently at it for three or four seconds.
2. He mentally projects the image to the receiver, and then consciously releases it. Releasing is done by thinking of something else. It's as if the sender is changing the TV channel; his mind switches to another thought and by doing so releases the image.
3. Continue until you've gone through the entire deck of twenty-five cards.

A correct guess by the receiver is classified as a hit. Anything higher than 20 percent hits indicates something more than chance. I am sure there are ways to cheat, but what is the point if you really want to develop your psychic awareness?

CARD SENSING EXERCISE

If you don't have access to a set of Zener cards, you can use a regular deck of playing cards instead. This exercise strengthens your ability to convey and receive telepathic messages and sharpens your intuitive skill.

1. Ask a friend or family member to assist you as a sender. Ask your assistant to shuffle a deck of ordinary playing cards, and then spread the cards face down on a table, while you, the receiver, relax with your eyes closed.

2. The sender draws a card. She holds the card facing her and focuses on the color on the card. The sender then asks you what color the card is.

3. Visualize the card in your mind's eye, concentrating upon the color, and say "red" or "black." Don't think about it too hard or second-guess yourself—respond with the first impression you receive.

4. If you are correct, the sender places the card on the right; if wrong, she places it to the left. The sender then draws another card and repeats the procedure.

5. Continue for as long as you like. How many did you get right? Did you actually see a color in your mind's eye? You might also get other impressions as well. Even if you don't get the color right, you may sense a heart or diamond shape, or a number. Record these hits, too.

6. Now, switch places so you become the sender while your partner assumes the role of receiver. Repeat the exercise. How did you do this time? Are you a better sender or receiver?

When the Psychical Research Foundation tested me using ESP cards, I did great the first few times. But by the third or fourth deck, my percentage of hits dropped dramatically. I believe this occurred because the process got boring. Parapsychologists call this "the decline effect." A similar decline occurs in other psychological experiments involving motivation, and could be attributed to mental fatigue. Because your mind will likely get bored or fatigued with repetition, don't do the same exercise over and over.

It's a good idea to keep a log or journal of your work. Note the conditions and length of time involved, as well as your results. You will improve with practice over time.

Telepathy and Emotional States

Telepathy appears to be strongly related to the individual's emotional state. The most spontaneous mind-to-mind communication occurs between loved ones, especially family members. Family members frequently finish one another's sentences or know what they are about to say before they say it. Mothers often display an uncanny ability to intuit what's going on with their children. Twins, particularly, seem to be able to read each other's minds.

How many of us, at one time or another, have suddenly bolted upright or stopped in our tracks, sensing that something traumatic had happened to a loved one? Start paying attention to impressions you receive that seem to come out of the blue. If possible, check them out to see if your perceptions were accurate. Keep a record of these telepathic occurrences. As you start paying attention to extrasensory communications, you may notice they become more frequent.

Sending and Receiving Telepathic Messages

As you've already discovered, some people are good senders—they excel at looking at an object or picture and forming an impression or message to transmit to someone else. Others achieve greater success as receivers and pick up impressions easily. What are some of the qualities or traits that distinguish the two? The sender must be capable of strong feelings, emotions, or thoughts in order to convey vivid impressions to the receiver. The sender must also be able to concentrate intensely. Without these attributes, any effort at telepathy will likely be unsuccessful.

A receiver, on the other hand, needs to maintain a relaxed state of consciousness and be open to the impressions the sender transmits. He shouldn't analyze, second-guess, or judge his perceptions. Nor should he try too hard. Testing over the years has underscored the value of heeding first impressions.

Telepathy may sound intimidating. It's not. Compare it to reading a new book: you just have to be willing to open your mind to its storyline or message. The simple truth is that we all have within us everything we need. Telepathy is not only possible, it happens all the time. You've undoubtedly experienced it already—now all you have to do is hone this psychic skill.

EMOTIONAL TELEPATHY EXERCISE

This exercise helps you develop your ability to connect with others telepathically. Keep in mind when you perform these exercises with friends and colleagues that there is no failing grade, no right or wrong, no good or bad. Your first impression is usually the right one. Record it or speak out, before your conscious mind has a chance to argue you out of it.

What's important is the adventure. You'll learn more about how your mind works and improve your understanding of your innate resources and potential. Commitment and trusting the process are important ingredients to your success.

1. Have a friend sit comfortably with her back to you.
2. Ask your friend to think of two different events, one at a time, that elicit strong feelings. One should be an unhappy event. The other should be something that thrills or excites her, something that brings a big smile. She shouldn't reveal what she's thinking at this stage. What's important are the feelings attached to the incidents. Feelings and emotions are critical in telepathic experiences and mind-to-mind communications.
3. As the receiver, see if you can feel the difference between the two mental messages conveyed by your friend. Which did you sense first—the happy or the sad experience? Did you feel the joy? The sadness? Did you sense anything else, such as images of people or environments?
4. Reverse roles and repeat this exercise. Practice the different roles several times.

Be patient, be persistent, and be peaceful. When you feel calm and relaxed, you are better able to receive and send signals telepathically—that's the reason for doing meditation and breathing exercises. And, as you would when developing any new skill, practice, practice, practice.

EXPERIMENTING WITH PICTURES

The next exercise involves sending and receiving pictures. Again, work with a friend or relative. One of you will be the sender, the other the receiver.

1. Select several photographs or other illustrations from magazines. Choose pictures that contain and convey lots of emotion. Try to avoid images that are too busy, however. In fact, one good choice for this exercise would be a child's coloring book—with or without colors added. These are usually simple drawings, easier to interpret at the end of the exercise.

2. Relax, perhaps by doing a few breathing exercises to center yourself.

3. First, take the role of sender. Focus on one of the pictures you've chosen and try to project an impression of the picture to your receiver. You might want to transmit an emotional feeling or physical sensation in addition to just the visual image. For instance, if the picture is of someone sitting in front of a fireplace, you could attempt to send a cozy feeling of warmth and comfort.

4. Examine the results. Did the receiver pick up the image you sent? In what form? As a color? As a shape? As an emotion or sensation? Many people expect that they will receive the whole picture; however, most do not.

5. Show your receiver several of the images and see if she can pick out which one you sent.

6. Repeat this exercise with three or four different images or pictures.

7. Switch places. The sender now becomes the receiver, and the receiver the sender.

8. Go through this process again and again. Be sure to select different pictures for each stage of the experiment.

Remember what I said about mental fatigue? Don't do these exercises to the point of exhaustion. On the other hand, it's important that you work on sending and receiving as often as possible. You might devote half an hour or so a few times a week. But don't just do the exercises. Let yourself be open to feeling what the people close to you are feeling. The real-life telepathic experience is what makes it all worthwhile.

When I was undergoing research at the Psychical Research Center in Durham, North Carolina, researchers sent me pictures from another room and asked me to write down my impressions. Sometimes all I saw was a flash of color. At other times, a shape or feeling came into my mind. Later, the researchers asked me to look at three or four pictures and pick which one I thought was being sent mentally to me. In some of the trials, it was difficult to see any similarities. Sometimes only one or two things stood out.

A panel of judges examined the images and/or feelings I had recorded on paper as having received during the trials, after which they looked at the same four pictures to determine if I had received the sent picture telepathically. More often than not, the judges could tell which picture I was receiving—whether as a flash of color, a form or series of forms, as an emotion, or all of the above.

Each of us perceives differently. You might receive impressions as pictures, colors, shapes, emotions, sensations, or something else. For example, when I'm describing the image of a murderer for the police, I see or receive only one specific detail of the killer's face at a time. The perpetrator's eye might emerge and then the eyebrow; next, a nose will appear, and then a mouth, and so on. I never see the whole face at once.

No one style of perceiving is better than any other. The more you work with these exercises and develop your own sending/receiving skills, the more confidence you'll have in your telepathic ability. You'll come to understand your own unique way of perceiving, and to distinguish when your impressions are correct and when they're not.

Improving Your Sending and Receiving Skills

With practice you can improve your telepathic abilities as both sender and receiver. The exercises in this book are designed to help you do just that. They're like practicing scales on the piano, in order to train yourself to eventually play Chopin's compositions. Here are some tips to keep in mind as you work.

Sending

As the sender, your job is to focus on whatever it is you intend to send. When sending pictures, try seeing each aspect of the image, as if you were describing it to an artist to draw. In addition to seeing the image, you also must learn to release it. This is part of the sending process. One simple way to do this is to shift your focus to something else when you've completed the transmission. This should be done quickly. Think of it in terms of throwing someone a ball. The throw is only completed when you release the ball.

Receiving

When you're practicing the role of the receiver, it's important to keep your mind open and relaxed. Try not to prejudge the situation or to have expectations of what will happen. Ask yourself questions such as: What colors am I getting? What shapes? What feelings? Don't put pressure on yourself to perform. There's no such thing as failure here, no reason to be shy or afraid. This is a healthy adventure of discovery, a chance to explore your own mind. And it's a lot of fun for you and companions who collaborate with you.

CHAPTER RECAP

Telepathy is the art of sending and receiving feelings, images, or thoughts from one person to another without any other cues or devices. Distance makes no difference. Many people experience telepathy in their everyday lives, although some are more open to such occurrences than others. Some people receive images of loved ones, either as passing thoughts while awake or in dreams. We may explain an event such as thinking of something at the same time as someone else by calling it a coincidence. If we finish someone else's sentence, we say this is because we know someone so well, we can guess what he is going to say. No matter what words we use to describe what has happened, some level of telepathy is present.

You can develop your own telepathic ability by practicing some of the same exercises that scientists use to study and define the phenomenon. Exploring what the mind can do enriches your life in countless ways.

CHAPTER 5

The Pendulum: Swinging, Swaying, and Spinning

"Most dowsers accept, quite happily, that they are moving the pendulum themselves. The point is that the subconscious mind causes these little tremors, not the conscious one. And so the movement of the pendulum can tell you what your intuition already knows, deep down."
—Teresa Moorey, *Magic House*

Using the pendulum is a form of dowsing. Although most people associate dowsing with hunting for water underground, this ancient technique uses intuition to search for anything that can't be discovered by the rational mind alone. Dowsers often employ a device such as a dowsing or divining rod, or a pendulum, to help them find water, metal ore, buried treasure, oil, or whatever else they're seeking. Long ago, folks held a forked tree branch shaped like a Y to dowse; now more sophisticated dowsing rods are available.

Interestingly, you don't have to actually walk the land holding a divining rod to dowse—you can simply use a pendulum to dowse a map. Betty Lundstead, former co-owner of Weiser Books, once used a pendulum this way to find an apartment in New York City and saved herself a lot of legwork. Some healers use a pendulum to locate and determine the cause of an illness.

Dowsing is an excellent way to tap information that resides in the unconscious, too, as you'll soon learn.

Many dowsing organizations and clubs exist—The American Society of Dowsers is the best known—and you'll find many good books on this subject. If dowsing is something you enjoy, or would like to explore in depth, you can join an organization or at least access the information these groups have compiled and shared.

Getting Started

Are you ready to give the pendulum a try? It is easy to make a hand-held pendulum. Take a chain about six to eight inches long and attach a ring to it. If you prefer, you can use a string with one or more fishing sinkers at one end, or you can purchase a ready-made pendulum at any New Age store. The appearance of the pendulum is not important.

Don't let other people use your pendulum or handle it. Your pendulum is very personal and should embody only your personality and carry your energy.

Hold the pendulum's chain or string lightly between your thumb and fingers. You can rest your elbow comfortably on a tabletop or other surface, allowing the pendulum's bob (the weight at the lower end) to dangle a couple of inches above the surface, or hold your arm bent slightly at the elbow as you allow the pendulum to do its thing. In general, I recommend that left-handed people use the right hand to hold the pendulum, and right-handed people should use the left hand, in order to access the less dominant side of the brain. However, this is not a universal rule; practice and feel which hand works best for you and consistently conveys to you correct information.

Stay relaxed when using the pendulum. That's important. You might want to meditate first. Clear your mind of concerns and distractions, and focus on what you want to know. The answers we seek are inside us. Using the pendulum allows you to connect with the hidden knowledge within you, to open the door and let the answers out to be received by you. But this cannot be achieved if your mind is cluttered or in turmoil. The more relaxed and peaceful your mind is, the better your chance of receiving a truthful answer to a question.

Establishing Yes and No Directions

Pendulums answer yes-or-no questions. Before using the pendulum to ask specific questions, you must first establish which direction the pendulum will swing for a yes answer and which direction for a no. This is specific to you. In other words, the yes and no directions are not the same for everyone.

To establish your yes direction, lightly grasp the pendulum's chain or string with one hand using as many fingers as you can. Hold it so the bob is above your other hand, which should be open and palm up. Ask the pendulum, "What is my yes direction?" Don't stare at the pendulum after you've asked this question (or any question). Close your eyes. When you feel the pendulum moving, open your eyes. The pendulum might swing back and forth, from side to side, in a clockwise circle, or in a counterclockwise circle. Whatever the response, that's the way your pendulum will swing for your yes answer.

Now find your no direction. Repeat the process above, but this time turn your other palm down and ask, "What is my no direction?"

You might have to do this several times before you know for certain what your yes and no directions are. Remember, you need to be relaxed. And for some people, that might be no easy challenge at first. This is new ground for you. Trust. Commit. Practice.

Taking a Test Run

Once you think you have your directions established, test them with simple questions whose answers you already know. For example, try asking such things as: "Is my name Mary?" "Do I live in Alaska?" "Do I have three legs?" "Am I a female?" Hold the pendulum away from other objects. (Holding the pendulum over your hand was only to establish your yes and no directions.)

If your name is Mary and the pendulum swings in the no direction, there is obviously something wrong. Are you relaxed? Is anything distracting you? Perhaps you need to go back and work again on establishing your true yes and no directions.

Once you are comfortable with the test results, you are ready to move on to the next stage: using the pendulum as an aid in your quest for answers.

How to Ask Your Questions

The pendulum can give one of three answers: yes, no, or maybe. What is this "maybe" response? Let's say your yes answer is the pendulum moving in a circle and your no answer is the pendulum swinging back and forth. If you ask a question that the pendulum cannot answer or that needs rephrasing, the pendulum may just stay still or move in a counterclockwise direction. This would be the maybe response. Think of it as your mind telling you, *Maybe yes, maybe no. Rephrase your question, please.*

Your intuitive mind responds best to simple but specific questions. For example, if you say, "Will it rain tomorrow?" your logical rational thinking mind knows you are talking about the city or town you live in, but your intuitive mind does not and will probably give you a yes answer: Yes, it will be raining somewhere tomorrow. The proper way to pose the question would be, "Will it rain tomorrow in Cleveland, Ohio?" (or wherever you live).

Pay attention to how your pendulum swings when you're alone and how it swings when you're with someone else. The presence of other people can change the flow of energy and influence the direction your pendulum moves. Consequently, it may give you an incorrect answer.

Various Uses for the Pendulum

Let's say you want to check for food allergies. When you have your breakfast, lunch, or dinner in front of you, place your pendulum over a specific food and ask, "Is this good for me?" You can do the same thing with vitamins; however, put your vitamins in individual envelopes so your logical mind can't interfere with your intuition. You might look at a vitamin C tablet and think logically, "I really need this," and your pendulum will swing yes. But if the vitamin C is in an envelope and out of sight, and you don't know which vitamin you're holding, then your intuitive mind has to take over.

You can use the pendulum to help you decide which movie or restaurant to go to. Ask the question, "Will I enjoy this movie, or this eatery?" You can also ask about parties, dates, or job applications. Will your baseball team win? Should you buy this house? Will your novel get published? Your possibilities are endless.

Sometimes I use the pendulum when searching for a missing person. I'm usually touching something that was left behind by the missing person, such as a toothbrush, hairbrush, or shoe. I need something very personal that no one else wore or used so I can connect to the missing person's energy.

If I'm sent a map, I usually turn it over so I will not be analyzing it with my logical mind. I divide the map in half, and then use my pendulum to see what side of the map the person is on. Then I cut that half into halves again and again, until I'm in one tiny spot. It's that spot I circle.

FIND YOUR KEYS

This exercise is both fun and practical. You can use the pendulum to find lost items. Try it the next time you misplace your keys (or glasses, cell phone, et cetera). Draw a map of the house, then hold the pendulum over a room in the drawing and ask if your keys are there now. The "now" is important because you might have had your keys in that room last week.

Once you determine which room the keys may be in, divide the room in half by drawing a line, and then pendulum dowse again. Repeat this by cutting the room into quarters, until you find your keys.

LOCATE A HIDDEN OBJECT

Do this exercise with a friend or family member. Leave the house while your assistant hides something (a jar of water or your wallet, for instance). When she's finished, return to the house and draw a map like the one you drew in the last exercise. Use the same technique described above for locating your keys. Let the pendulum help you find the hidden object.

GUESS WHAT'S IN THE CONTAINERS

Here's another dowsing exercise you can do with a friend or family member. Get some containers and collect items that can be categorized as either manmade or natural. Close your eyes while your assistant places one item in each container.

Hold the pendulum above each container individually and ask, "Is what's inside this container natural?" Write down your answer, and then put the container aside. Do the same with the other containers. When you've finished, go back and see how well you scored.

WHAT'S WRITTEN ON THE PAPERS?

This exercise prevents your rational mind from influencing the pendulum's motion. On slips of paper, write down several personal questions similar to those you used to test your pendulum's directions, such as, "Is my name Mary?" "Do I live in Alaska?" and so on. Throw in one or two trick questions, such as, "Am I a parakeet?" or "Do I live on the moon?" Fold the papers so they're all the same size. Put the papers in a bowl and mix them up.

Remove one of the papers with one hand. Hold the pendulum in the other hand and ask, "Is what's written on this paper true?" After the pendulum gives you a yes or no response, write the pendulum's answer on the outside of the paper and put it aside. Then repeat the process until all the papers have been dowsed. Afterward, open the papers to see how your intuitive mind has responded.

Your questions can be asked aloud or silently. As you become more proficient in using your pendulum, you won't even have to ask the question—the pendulum will move in one direction or the other and give you the answer immediately.

Don't keep asking the same question again and again; this shows doubt. Wait at least a few weeks or a month before repeating your question. Over time, the answer may change as circumstances change. Sometimes we get an answer we don't like. That doesn't mean it's wrong. It's just an answer we didn't want to hear.

SENSE WHAT'S IN THE ENVELOPES

Have a friend or family member place certain items in envelopes —don't look while he's doing this. It's important that you not be able to guess at what's in an envelope just by the shape or size. Ask him to number the items. Here are a few suggestions of what to put in the envelopes. Don't restrict yourself to this list, however. Use your imagination and be creative.

- Money
- Vitamin C capsule
- Dirt from the garden or yard
- Cat or dog hair
- Sugar
- Salt
- Tobacco
- Coffee

Use the pendulum to ask specific questions about each hidden item. Remember, these must be yes-or-no questions. Ask one or more questions for each envelope. For instance, you could ask, "Is this good for me?" or "Do I like this?"

DOWSING COLORS

You did this exercise earlier to see if you could sense the energies of colors. Now let's see how you do with a pendulum. Place four green sheets of paper into four opaque envelopes, then put one red sheet of paper in an identical fifth envelope. Mix them up well, so you don't know which envelope contains the red paper. See if you can pick the red one by using your pendulum. If that is too difficult, try using only two envelopes with green sheets of paper and one envelope with red paper in it. (You can use any color paper; they don't have to be red and green.)

WHERE'S THE MONEY?

You will need four quarters and one dime for this exercise. Ask a friend or family member to place a paper cup over each coin. Hold the pendulum above one cup at a time, and try to pick out the dime. Your pendulum should answer yes or no.

FIND THE FORGERY

Write your name on four identical pieces of paper. Then have someone else write your name on an identical piece of paper. Fold them all equally and mix them up. Try to find the forgery with your pendulum. How did you do?

Why Use the Pendulum?

Using the pendulum isn't just an amusing game; it can help you discover things about yourself. For instance, let's say you pick up a box, ask if what's inside is good for you, get a no response from the pendulum, and then open the box and find money. Is this an incorrect response? Or does it suggest that, unconsciously, you're still under the influence of something your parents or another authority figure might have instilled in you regarding money? Perhaps when you were a child they drummed into you the oft-used adage that the love of money is the root of all evil.

By unconsciously believing this, you could be erecting a mental block that prevents money and financial success from entering your life. Realizing this lets you discover something about yourself, past and present. This new awareness will allow you to counter your unconscious attitude toward money and start to see it as a tool. You'll now reach your own conclusions about money and prosperity.

The pendulum can help us understand many things about ourselves, our lifestyles, and our priorities. Be prepared for some revealing developments, even challenging ones. But, again, enjoy the quest for discovery and truth. Remember, the uses for your pendulum are limited only by your imagination and curiosity.

INTUITING INFORMATION ABOUT STRANGERS

Here is another way you can use your pendulum to gain information and improve your sensing ability. You don't personally need to intellectually know information to get the correct answers. Have a friend or family member bring you something personal, perhaps a pen or a piece of jewelry, belonging to a person you don't know. Ask questions, such as the following ones, about the individual to whom the object belongs. Use your pendulum to provide yes or no answers.

1. Does this person own a dog now?
2. Does this person own a cat now?
3. Does this person live in an apartment now?

4. Does this person live in a house now?
5. Does this person have a brother now?
6. Does this person have a sister now?
7. Does this person like gardening?
8. Does this person like cooking?
9. Is this person mechanically inclined?
10. Does this person live with another person at this time?
11. Does this person like to drink beer?
12. Does this person like to drink wine?
13. Does this person like to hunt?
14. Does this person work out regularly?

Although we usually pick up vibes better from people we know well or to whom we're related, this exercise shows that you can also intuit information about total strangers with your pendulum. That's why I use this technique when I'm working with police to solve missing persons cases and violent crimes.

AVIATION TEST

This exercise demonstrates that your pendulum can provide answers to questions even if your rational mind can't. Ronald F. Conroy, veteran air traffic controller, contributed the following specialized aviation questions that few people would be able to answer using logic and rational thinking alone. But your intuitive mind has access to information your logical one doesn't. Using your pendulum, see how many of these questions you can answer correctly. The answers follow the series of questions; don't peek until after you've used your pendulum to answer them!

1. The ATCSCC in Herndon, Virginia, regulates the flow of air traffic for all the major airports in the United States.
2. A Boeing 757 has four jet engines.
3. A vector is a specific magnetic heading issued to a pilot.
4. The standard rate of turn for an aircraft moving faster than 250 knots is 1.5 degrees per second.
5. ASDE-X Radar is Air Surveillance Detection Equipment.
6. Propylene glycol is a type of jet fuel.
7. A radar altimeter (RA) measures the distance above sea level.
8. The Radar Approach Control facility only controls aircraft on approach to the airport.
9. The Airbus A-380 is the largest aircraft in the world.
10. English is the language for aviation communication worldwide.

Answers to Aviation Test:
1. Yes
2. No
3. Yes
4. Yes
5. No
6. No
7. No
8. No
9. Yes
10. Yes

CHAPTER RECAP

Using the pendulum is a form of dowsing. It's an excellent way to tap information that resides in the unconscious. The pendulum's aesthetic appearance is not important. You can use a pendulum to help you understand things about yourself—your health, lifestyle, attitudes, and beliefs—as well as about other people. Your pendulum can also assist you in making both minor and major decisions, when your rational mind cannot.

CHAPTER 6

Affirmation and Visualization

"This is your life, are you where you want to be?"

—Jonathan Foreman

Affirmation says "yes" to the best in you and around you. Visualization is a mental technique for imagining and creating your own reality, popularized by Shakti Gawain in the 1970s. Both affirmation and visualization can be used to awaken your psychic abilities and explore your mind's full potential. By training your mind, these techniques enable you to reprogram your limited thinking, eliminate old beliefs, expand possibilities, and bring about the conditions you desire in your life. They partner with you in reaching new heights and allowing your own uniqueness to flourish.

A Closer Look at Affirmation

Affirmation is a form of self-programming the mind. An affirmation is a short, positive statement worded in the present tense, as if the desired condition already exists. It sets the stage for fulfilling your needs and desires. Regularly saying an affirmation aloud, thinking it to yourself, and/or reading it written on a piece of paper can dramatically affect your thought processes and your beliefs.

Using an affirmation is like programming a computer, except you're programming your mind. What you put into it is your choice. You have control. The better you know yourself and your needs, the easier it becomes to program the mind for what you want it to believe. Your mind listens to whatever you put into it. To believe is to become. Realizing this puts you on the road toward reaching your full potential and power. The more you are able to connect with the underdeveloped parts of your mind, the closer you come to awakening and empowering your psychic awareness.

Repetition Creates Belief

Much of what you think and believe today comes from having heard or read it often throughout your life, and your beliefs motivate you to behave in certain ways. Your parents continually telling you that you'd never get ahead if you didn't get an education, for instance, may have spurred you to graduate from college with honors. Repeatedly hearing that it's better to give than to receive might have interfered with your ability to save money or become financially prosperous. One reason people use affirmations is to undo old programming they wish to be rid of and to replace it with new beliefs that will help them achieve their present objectives.

Repetition is at the heart of affirming. The more you repeat, the more likely you will believe. When you repeat something over and over again, you touch on the science of thought, a study as ancient as humankind. Wise men throughout the ages have known about the power of the mind. *What you believe yourself to be, you are,* is both a personal and a universal message. In Mark

9:23, Jesus tells us, "Everything is possible for the person who believes." More than two millennia ago, the Buddha said, "All that we are is the result of what we have thought."

Your Beliefs Create Your Reality

What appears as coincidence may simply be the working out of a pattern you started with your own thoughts. I believe psychics can see and/or feel what your future holds by picking up on the thoughts and emotions you send out, both consciously and unconsciously. Your fears, hates, loves, and desires produce energy. Those emotions attract similar energy into your life. I've discussed this before, but it bears repeating: What you believe about yourself and your life becomes a reality. Nothing happens by accident. There is mental energy behind everything in your life, significant or trivial. In the arena of human life, we set up these causes and create these effects with our own thinking.

When the conscious mind wants something, it uses the power of reason to attain it. The brain collects and analyzes the data. A conscious decision suggests self-awareness and active attention. On the other hand, the subconscious has no reasoning power; it simply accepts what it is told. It will work just as diligently to attract the negative as the positive. Giving it an affirmation directs it to attain whatever you state. In this way, you use your thoughts and words intentionally to create your reality.

Experimenting with Affirmations

Let's design an effective affirmation. Think of something you wish to change or attract into your life. Maybe your goal is to attract money. Instead of saying, "I don't have to worry about money anymore," say, "I now have plenty of money for everything I desire." The first statement focuses on a negative: worrying about money. The second highlights the positive: having plenty of money.

Structure your affirmations with care. Use strong, powerfully positive messages. Edit out all negative words such as *no, can't, not, don't,* and *never.* When I first learned about this approach, it was a revelation. I had no idea that the mind seizes upon emotions such as worry, fear, and anger. I was also surprised to learn that, even when the affirmation is positive in direction ("I will not smoke") adding a negative word ("not") is counterproductive. The subconscious ignores the qualifying words such as *won't, never,* and *not,* and hears only the operative word *smoke.*

EMPHASIZE THE POSITIVE

At a job I used to have, I felt ridiculed and undermined by one particular individual. Although this upset me, I was determined not to get angry the next time I had a meeting with this person. I prepared myself by repeatedly stating, "I won't get angry. I won't get upset. I won't be irritated during the meeting." But it didn't work. My nemesis barely had finished saying something disagreeable before I exploded.

I was devastated because my approach had not worked. I quickly made an appointment with a hypnotist I'd worked with before to resolve a health issue, in order to find out what I had done wrong. He kindly explained that the subconscious only recognizes and acknowledges key words such as those I'd used: *angry, upset,* and *irritated.* Thereafter, I only gave myself positive suggestions. I affirmed I was calm and relaxed. The switch from negative to positive worked.

Use the Present Tense

The same hypnotist taught me something else that was equally important: affirmations should always be framed in the present tense. Saying "I will be rich" expresses a future situation. Consequently, your subconscious doesn't feel a need to act on this command right away; all it has to do is acknowledge that the situation exists at some unspecified time in the future. And the situation will remain that way forever. For this reason, always express affirmations in the present tense, as if the conditions they describe were already a reality. For example:

- I am calm at meetings.
- I am a happy person.
- I am a loving person and attract loving people into my life.
- I have the perfect job.
- I attract financial success.

Effective Affirmations

Be honest with yourself, though. Don't tell yourself that you aren't sick when you obviously are. Instead, suggest that your body is healing and becoming healthier. Repeat affirmative statements such as, "My back and neck are growing healthier and stronger every day. They are healing and strengthening by the hour."

If you're trying to lose weight, your affirmation might be something like, "I'm getting thinner and healthier every day. I'm losing weight. My desire for food is diminishing." Repeat this statement often.

Maybe you want to be more relaxed during the day. Your affirmation could be something like, "I'm more and more relaxed every hour, every day. I'm so peaceful and relaxed. I now feel good inside and out. I am at peace."

Don't overload your subconscious. Work on changing one situation or condition at a time. Use simple, concise language in formulating and stating your affirmations, Using an appropriate adjective or adverb will make the suggestion come alive; for example, "I am radiantly healthy" or "I am blissfully happy in my marriage." This makes it real, and more desirable. When you state your affirmations, be sure to express them with as much positive emotion as you can muster.

Viva Variety

Ideally, the mind should be reprogrammed weekly with a different message and goal. Or, reword your message and present it from a different angle. For instance, instead of saying "I'm more and more relaxed every hour, every day" day after day, you might shift to "Everything I do flows smoothly and easily. I'm content with every aspect of my day." If you constantly repeat the same affirmation, the mind tends to stop listening. Maybe it gets bored. Maybe it's like a teenager who tunes out when you become repetitive. Remember how your mother told over and over to not slam the screen door? You just stopped listening to her after a while.

Vary your positive messages. Your mind is infinitely curious and thrives on challenges. To keep it intrigued, give it new things to consider and make the action interesting. If the subconscious is kept on its toes, it will do as you say.

If you feel a need to refer to the past, you might word your affirmation in a manner similar to this one: "I am more calm and patient with my coworkers than I used to be." If you're preparing for something that will happen in the near future, such as a business conference, try structuring the affirmation like this: "At next week's meeting I am confident, calm, and in control."

Tips for Creating Successful Affirmations

Avoid setting unrealistic goals. Be reasonable in forming your affirmations. Don't suggest something you don't really think is possible or is downright ridiculous, such as "Ben Affleck is in love with me" or "Courtney Cox wants my body." It sounds great, but your subconscious will know you're just fooling around and won't really believe what you say.

Write your affirmations down and be sure to personalize them. Your affirmations should be designed to change things in yourself, not to change other people.

How many affirmations should you come up with during the time frame of a week? I recommend no more than four or five, which all address the same objective. Then repeat them over and over. For instance, you might formulate four or five different affirmations about attracting wealth and state these often throughout the week.

The next week you might switch to a different subject, perhaps love. Formulate four or five love affirmations. Use these throughout the day for a week. Remember to always state your affirmations in the present tense and indicate the end result you seek, not the steps necessary to get there.

Affirmation Checklist

Just to make sure you've covered all your bases, let's go through the following checklist for designing successful affirmations. As you begin to see your affirmations and intentions take shape in your life, you'll gain a greater appreciation for how your mind works and for its amazing abilities. You'll come to trust the power of your mind and feel more confident using it in ways beyond the ordinary, accepted channels.

1. **Be specific.** Write your affirmations down in detail, but be brief. Use the present tense.
2. **Be positive.** Negative thoughts and energy slam the door, shutting out your dreams. Negative is poison. Positive is power.
3. **Be persistent.** Everything takes time. You never get anywhere by giving up.
4. **Release.** The only way to release is to believe. A common thread runs through many spiritual teachings and makes them work for those who sincerely accept and apply the teachings. That common thread is belief. An old Latin proverb says, "Believe that you have it and you have it."

A Closer Look at Visualization

When you engage in visualization, you create a picture in your mind of something, particularly something that you feel will enhance your life. It's a type of imagination, but a directed type with specific goals. It's not the same as aimless daydreaming or escapist fantasizing.

Many people use visualization in connection with meditation. I spoke earlier about using the imagery of waves breaking on the beach in order to facilitate relaxation during meditation. That's an example of visualization.

Like affirmation, visualization can be used to change old beliefs, ideas, habits, and emotions, and to reprogram your mind to bring about outcomes you desire. Often affirmations and visualizations are used together to increase the effectiveness of both. Developing your visualization skill also expands your brain's capabilities, especially in the areas of imagination, creativity, and intuition. Therefore, you can also strengthen your psychic potential by practicing visualization.

Healing with Visualization

Some years ago, I was involved in several auto accidents that caused me to be hospitalized with back and neck injuries that only got worse despite treatment. The doctors finally said there was nothing else they could do and that I would have to learn to live with the pain. I was young and didn't want to be in pain for the rest of my life. I wasn't about to give up. I visited a hypnotist and explained both my dilemma and my resolve. I learned self-hypnotism to ease the pain in my neck and back.

I visualized myself being perfect. I saw and felt the ailments and pain easing their tight grip. I visualized myself walking, working, and moving about with increased ease. I affirmed this by repeatedly telling my body how perfect it was and how good I felt. This took some time, but eventually it worked and I was pain free.

Training Yourself with Visualizations

Athletes often visualize themselves playing their sport as a way to discipline their minds so they perform better. Shortly before competing in the 2010 Olympics, Canadian alpine snowboarder Michael Lambert spoke to the Canadian press and revealed one of his secrets to success: he uses visualization as part of his regular training program. "I think it really helped train my mind, gave me more control over it," he explained.

In his book *Hedge Fund Masters: How Hedge Fund Traders Set Goals, Overcome Barriers, and Achieve Peak Performance*, Ari Kiev described an experiment involving three separate basketball teams. One team was directed to practice on a basketball court in the usual manner. Another team was told not to practice at all. The third team was instructed to visualize playing. For several weeks, all three teams repeated their assigned routines daily. At the end of the experiment, results showed the team that actually practiced on the court and the group that only visualized playing improved at about the same rate. The do-nothing team did not improve. Team members who visualized shooting baskets saw themselves scoring and doing well. Their visualizations told their subconscious minds to do well. Once they got on the court and competed, indeed they showed improvement and played well.

Athletes aren't the only ones who can benefit from visualization. Everyone can. Whatever skill you wish to develop or whatever goal you wish to achieve, you can increase your chances of success through the use of visualization. For instance, if you have an important business meeting coming up, close your eyes and imagine yourself expressing your ideas clearly, intelligently, and calmly. Envision your colleagues listening attentively and appreciatively to you. If you're taking a test, visualize yourself confidently answering all the questions correctly and scoring an A. If you're going out on a big date, see yourself having a wonderful time, looking terrific, enjoying lively conversation, and so on. Always imagine the good things you desire taking place, as vividly as you possibly can.

Incorporating Emotions into Your Visualizations

Thoughts create feelings and feelings fuel your thoughts. Emotions give your thoughts energy, depth, meaning, and motivation. Emotions usually accompany your experiences. When you include emotion in your visualizations, you enrich them. You imbue them with authenticity and hence increase their power. The more you truly believe the visualization is real, the more quickly you'll accomplish your goal.

Because of this, it's important to bring feelings into your visualizations. Don't just see a picture, *experience* the picture. Get all your senses involved. If you're visualizing dining in a gourmet restaurant, savor the smells and tastes. If you're imagining a vacation at the beach, feel the sun warming your body, the sand beneath your feet, your happiness at being in a beautiful and relaxing place. Really get into it.

Consider feeling, visualizing, and affirming as an interlocking triad—each reinforces the others. Like three strands of a rope woven together, they connect you to your goal. Visualize it, affirm it, and feel it. See! Say! Savor! Whatever the mind can conceive and believe, it can achieve.

Tips for Creating Successful Visualizations

Your subconscious doesn't distinguish between reality and imagination. To the subconscious, visualization is the same as experiencing actual events. That's why you always want to create visualizations of things you truly want to happen, and steer your mind away from thoughts of things you don't want to happen.

Enrich your visualizations with as many vibrant, pleasant sensations and details as possible—and always put yourself in the picture. If your objective is to acquire a new car, for instance, see yourself driving the exact model car you want. Smell the leather seats. Hear the engine roar to life as you press the accelerator. Feel the steering wheel in your hands. See yourself smiling and enjoying the ride.

Many people find it easier to envision active scenes than passive ones. Imagine yourself running the football into the end zone for the winning touchdown instead of just seeing the final score on the scoreboard.

To avoid boredom, vary your visualizations regularly, just as you did with your affirmations. If you're visualizing a dream vacation, create several different "movies" of what you'll do on your vacation—basking on the beach, eating in terrific restaurants, shopping in wonderful stores, dancing under the stars—and enjoy every minute of it.

Maybe you don't think you're very good at visualizing. If that's the case, it's okay to prime the pump. Find a picture in a magazine that depicts something you want—a house, car, vacation, or whatever. If your goal is to lose weight, it might be a picture of a body that looks the way you want yours to look. Cut out the picture and gaze at it every morning for several moments. Use your imagination to perfect an image of the object, person, or situation. Get your emotions involved. Experience it. Feel yourself and the picture merging: you aren't merely an outsider viewing a photograph, put yourself *in* the picture.

VISUALIZATION EXERCISE

This meditation helps to strengthen your imagination, creativity, and intuition through the use of visualization. Before you start, choose a color you want to use in this meditation. (You may want to refer back to the list of color associations in Chapter 2.)

After you have done your breath work and your breathing is slow, deep, and steady, inhale and visualize a small cloud of the color you've chosen floating above your head. As you exhale, feel the cloud descend until it surrounds your head and shoulders, and then let it melt into your body. Each time you inhale, re-create a colorful cloud above your head. As you exhale, allow the cloud to drift down and surround you with its color. You may experience sensations or emotions associated with the color. For instance, blue might have a calming or cooling effect on you, whereas red might make you feel energized or warm. Do this exercise for ten minutes at a time.

YOU ARE MORE THAN YOUR BODY

This visualization exercise is designed to help you experience yourself as more than the physical body with which you ordinarily identify. It helps you become aware of your aura and the energy field that is also a part of you. At the same time, it expands your psychic awareness of the space around you and increases your sensitivity to it.

1. Make sure you won't be disturbed for at least ten to fifteen minutes. Turn off the phone and the TV; put a Do Not Disturb sign on the door if necessary.
2. Lie on your back, in a place where you feel comfortable. Close your eyes and take a few slow, deep breaths to relax.
3. When you are ready, turn your attention to the top of your head. Imagine a white light extending out from the top and sides of your head, like a halo, radiating outward about six inches or so. This is your aura, the vital energy field I talked

about earlier that surrounds your body. Hold this image in your mind for a few moments as you try to sense feeling in your aura. You might experience a tingling sensation, tickling, warmth, sensitivity, or some other feeling—or perhaps nothing at all.

4. After a few moments, imagine your aura contracting so that it fits snugly against your head, like a cap.

5. Next, turn your attention to your feet. Imagine white light extending out from the soles of your feet about six inches or so. Again, this is your aura. Hold this image in your mind for a few moments as you try to sense feeling in your aura. You might experience a tingling sensation, tickling, warmth, sensitivity, or some other feeling—or perhaps nothing at all.

6. After a few moments, imagine your aura contracting again until it fits close to your feet, like a pair of socks.

7. Repeat this visualization two more times, first focusing your attention on your head and then on your feet. Each time, try to project your aura out a little further and hold it there for a little longer.

8. When you are comfortable with this practice, imagine expanding your entire body outward in all directions, about six inches or so. You are now completely surrounded by a bubble of white light. Notice any sensations that exist in your aura: tingling, tickling, warmth, sensitivity, or anything else. You might become aware of how your own energy field interacts with the energy in your environment and pick up vibes you never noticed before. Your aura may feel like a second skin, but expanded out from your physical body, as if your body were swelling like a balloon. Whatever you feel—or don't feel—is okay.

9. After a while, withdraw your aura so it fits comfortably against your body again.

10. Repeat the expanding process two more times, and each time try to send your aura out a little further. Then contract it again.

11. Relax and breathe slowly, deeply for a few moments. Then allow your breathing to return to normal. When you're ready, open your eyes.

Combining Affirmations with Visualizations

Just as training with weights strengthens your body's muscles, training with affirmations and visualizations strengthens your creative and intuitive muscles. By combining affirmations with visualizations, you increase their effectiveness exponentially.

Using the guidelines discussed above, design an affirmation that clearly and succinctly states the outcome you seek. For example, if you want to lose weight and get in shape physically, you could say, "My body grows slimmer, stronger, and healthier every day." Then create a mental picture that depicts the body you'd like to have. Be realistic, though. If you're fifty years old, five feet two inches tall, and big-boned, you probably won't end up looking like a supermodel, and your underlying doubt might actually sabotage your attempts.

Meditate daily for ten minutes, envisioning yourself as slim and healthy. At the same time, mentally repeat these words: "My body grows slimmer, stronger, and healthier every day." Feel what it's like to be slimmer, stronger, and healthier. Enjoy getting compliments from other people, buying beautiful new clothes that look great on you, moving gracefully and comfortably, and so on.

You could also cut out a magazine picture of a body that resembles the one you'd like to have and write your affirmation across the picture. Position the picture where you'll see it often in order to mentally reinforce your goal.

CHAPTER RECAP

Affirmations and visualizations enable you to program your mind and change your reality in both the present and the future. Affirmations are positive statements that describe an outcome you desire. Visualizations are mental pictures you create that depict an outcome you desire. Your subconscious perceives the images and statements you present to it as commands, and will endeavor to bring them about. Combining the two techniques increases their effectiveness exponentially. Because both practices tap the creative and intuitive part of your mind, they also strengthen your intuition when you do them regularly.

CHAPTER 7

Attract Anything or Anyone

"The possibility of stepping into a higher plane is quite real for everyone. It requires no force or effort or sacrifice. It involves little more than changing our ideas about what is normal."

—Deepak Chopra

In the previous chapter, I talked about using affirmations and visualizations as tools for meditation, healing, releasing unwanted habits and conditions, and improving situations in your life. These techniques let you connect with the intuitive part of your brain in order to bring about the changes you seek.

Change must occur at a deep, intuitive level in order to be effective in the long term, not just at the rational, conscious level where we usually function as we go about our daily activities. Just saying or thinking we'd like to change something in our lives isn't enough. Practices such as meditation, visualization, and affirmation, which enable us to tap in to the subconscious levels of our minds where old patterns are stored, can help you to fundamentally revise and re-create yourself according to your vision of what you want to be and to accomplish *now*.

Use Your Psychic Power to Attract the Relationship You Desire

As a professional psychic, I have come in contact with many men and women who are successful, attractive, and pleasant, but who are without a significant life partner with whom to share their journeys. Some openly lament this void; others try to hide it, adding to the intensity of their anguish.

BE CAREFUL WHAT YOU WISH FOR

When I first became interested in psychic phenomena and started putting my knowledge to work, I used to sit in a nightclub night after night practicing psychometry with willing and interested clientele. Psychometry, as you'll recall, is the practice of intuitively picking up vibrations and information from an object such as a watch or ring. Every night, I observed people coming into the club where they engaged in the age-old mating dance, and I watched their games unfold.

Being a single woman myself, I became curious to see what the visualization techniques I'd read about might achieve for me, and decided to put them to the test. What a bonus it would be if I used my psychic ability to change my lifestyle and attract a new man into my life. If nothing else, I figured the research would be useful in my work.

The first thing I had to decide was what kind of man I wanted. In this nightclub I had watched many happy couples dancing by my table, and I decided I certainly wanted someone who could dance splendidly. I also chose to see my partner as drop-dead handsome, with intelligence and quick wit stirred in, of course. The final ingredient in the mix was sensitivity—I wanted to conjure up a gentle kind of soul. Ah, now *that* was a pleasant visualization!

Soon a waitress placed a glass of wine in front of me, courtesy of a happy client, and my thoughts were interrupted. It was like being stirred from a joyful dream. I snapped back into the vibrant environment of the nightclub and thought no more about my handsome man visualization. I let it go.

During a slow evening at the nightclub a few weeks later, a good-looking man approached my table and asked me to dance. I had been a bit bored so I leaped at the invitation. I found myself in the arms of an excellent dancer as we dipped, twirled, and swirled around the floor—I felt like Cinderella at the ball. When we finished dancing, he sat at my table and we talked on through the evening. We laughed at everything and at nothing. His gentle sensitivity was extremely endearing. He seemed aware of my feelings, and genuinely cared. He was also clearly intelligent.

Unfortunately, I had left out a very important part of my visualization: romance and sex. He was everything I had visualized, but my handsome man was gay! Let me quickly add that I have no bias against gay people. This man was a wonderful person. I have the highest respect for him and a joyful memory of our dancing, conversation, and time together. But the experience brought home to me the meaning of the old expression "be careful what you wish for." It also clearly showed me that my psychic powers could attract whatever I wanted: all I had to do was envision it.

Phooey, I thought, I'll just include sex in the next visualization. So I did, but I neglected to repeat the complete visualization process that included the other qualities I was seeking. This time I had left out sensitivity, intelligence, and looks.

What happened? The next man that pounced into my life was very macho and aggressive, lunging at me and clutching my body. To him, I was only a thing, an object. Yikes!

I decided to put the "man visualization" experiment on hold until I really knew what I wanted and needed. I realized, too, that I had grasped something significant about using my powers of visualization, and needed to respect that potential.

As you visualize what you want for yourself and the changes you intend to bring about in the future, be aware that the subconscious doesn't analyze the directions you give it. Nor does it make assumptions or read anything into what you say. It's absolutely literal. It will bring you exactly what or whom you visualize. Know who you are, know what you want—then create it!

The scenarios are unlimited. Let's review a few examples. You may only be looking for a weekend romance at this stage in your life. You want an abundance of sexual pleasure for both of you, but no ties, no commitments. Maybe you desire a fling with someone incredibly wealthy, good-looking, and sensitive. Or you may be looking for a cottage-and-picket-fence marriage. You might be longing for a deep, satisfying relationship that will last a lifetime. Perhaps you want none of the above and seek something and someone entirely different from what I've described. That's fine. But before you start the process of attracting someone into your life, decide what you *really* want.

Whether your objective is to find the ideal relationship, get a better job, attract money, or improve your health, tapping your intuition gives you the edge. Intuition is the ultimate creative tool. It has played a role in many of the great achievements and advances in history. For example, Jonas Salk, who discovered the polio vaccine, believed intuition aided him in his work and he wrote a book about it titled *Anatomy of Reason: Merging of Intuition and Reason.* According to Dr. Salk, "Intuition will tell the thinking mind where to look next."

Determine what you most desire and be completely clear about what you ask for, so you can fulfill your dream. The creative and psychic ability is there, but it needs guidance from your rational mind to establish the parameters and check all the boxes. When both parts of your brain work together in this way, you can attract anything and everything you truly want.

Three Keys to Attracting What You Want

Remember, your thoughts and feelings send out energy that attracts people and situations that are on the same wavelength as you. Like attracts like. Ask yourself what brings you pleasure, peace, and happiness. Are you always trying to please other people? Have you stopped looking for what makes you happy? Are you just settling for whatever comes your way? If so, perhaps it's time to open new doors and be brave enough to step through them, to start discovering who you are today.

In order to attract what you want, you need to incorporate three fundamentals in your life: desire, effort, and belief.

Desire

Get in touch with your own needs. Really know and understand what you want, not what society says you should want or what someone else wants. Deference to others makes you wishy-washy and undermines who you truly are. When you know unequivocally what you desire in your life (be it a new car, a new job, a better relationship, or spiritual growth), you can visualize it with total clarity.

Once you're clear about what you want, marshal your passion and fuel your objective with it. The more you desire something and the more emotion you invest in your dream, the faster it will come to fruition.

Effort

Forget waving the magic wand or concocting magic potions. Instead, commit yourself to accomplishing your goals and strive for what you want. Devote 100 percent of your effort toward achieving your goal. When all your energy is concentrated, you cannot fail. A Greek philosopher once said, "The moment that we commit the universe conspires to assist us." It's as basic and as complex as that.

Belief

If you believe in yourself and in your efforts, nothing can stand in your way for long. As Henry Ford once said, "Whether you think you can or think you can't—you are right." Whenever you visualize, believe with all your heart that your visualization will materialize. The mind isn't just powerful, it is the *only* power.

An Amazingly Effective Visualization Program

The three-day visualization program that follows offers a wonderful technique for making changes happen. It enables you to create and attract in abundance whatever you most desire. Getting what you want isn't that difficult. *Knowing* what you want is more complex. You can use this program to change any situation in your life—your work, personal relationships, health, and so on.

Simply adapt the steps described in this section so they suit your objectives.

Let's say, for instance, your wish is to draw a life partner to you. As you begin this special three-day visualization, make sure you specify exactly what kind of person you want. Imagine this person carefully. Remember my experience with the handsome dancer? To do this, you must have a clear understanding of yourself and what you need. Pay attention to your own values and tastes when you enter into this three-day visualization. It's you who will be involved with this person, after all, so design your vision to complement your own romantic essence and personality. Make sure you visualize the person as single, divorced, or widowed.

Sure, there are numerous dating services available. The Internet offers countless match-up options, available for a fee. Some claim sensational results and I'm sure many people have found these services helpful. But I believe the visualization program detailed here is the best, the most personal, and the most powerful approach. It's also the safest in these days of identity theft and Internet predators. Stalkers and predators can draw personal information off the Internet or Facebook or a blog, track you down, and then make your life miserable. Using my exercises, you don't send files of information about yourself to an unknown third party, to be stored who knows where. Hackers cannot compromise or invade your visualizations. Your imagination is completely confidential. Only the person who's right for you, who's on the same wavelength as you, will connect with your visualization.

Ready? Let's begin.

Getting Started

Commit to practicing this technique for three days. Whenever your daily routine allows you some free time—while you're washing the dishes, stopped at a traffic light, or involved in any mundane task—you're going to visualize the person you wish to attract. First, relax, really relax—and then relax some more. Trust. Yield to relaxation. Don't be wary, dubious, or hesitant. Feel confident and secure about the steps you are ready to take. This may be new to you, but if you open up to it, go with its flow, the experience will be a rewarding one.

Think of yourself as an artist sculpting a highly sought-after masterpiece. You start with a cold hard lump of clay, then you pat it and knead it until it becomes workable enough to shape and mold. Visualize the person you're sculpting as you smooth the rough surfaces, carefully defining every inch of your creation to perfection.

Start with the physical aspects of the desired person, as these are often the easiest to imagine. Each of us has ideas about what physical characteristics the perfect man or woman might have, and this is your opportunity to actualize your ideals. See his or her eyes, mouth, hair, body, and so forth as clearly as you can. Look at photographs in magazines if you want to stimulate the visualization process.

Refining Your Vision

Next, visualize a moving picture of how that person treats you when you are together, whether it's just the two of you or when you're in the company of others. Do you like lots of hugs and affection? If so, feel the warmth of the hugs and your body's response to them. Visualize how sharing affection with this person makes you feel. Get your emotions and your senses involved in the visualization.

Now think of things you'd like to share with this person. Do you want him or her to enjoy cooking? Feel the delight that comes from preparing an exquisite meal that culminates in enjoying a romantic dinner together. See the person in the kitchen, and the two of you laughing and sampling food items. Smell the rich aromas of the herbs and spices. Use all five of your senses in your visualization; the greater the amount of detail the better. You might see vivid images or a colorful scenario unfold before you— even smell the scents. Perhaps you'll experience strong feelings. Everyone's reaction is unique and different.

Visualize your dream-come-true very clearly, adding the smallest of details. If you have difficulty doing this, try to remember when you were very young and loved to daydream. Remember how easily this daydreaming came and how enjoyable it was. Have fun and enjoy your visualization for the next three days.

Spend as much time as you like experiencing this image, seeing it fulfilled in your mind and in your heart. Visualize yourself going out with the person for whatever sort of evening you'd enjoy. See yourselves together in places you like to be, and let the night evolve for a while. Now visualize yourself at this person's home. What kind of place does he/she live in? How does he/she entertain you? Experience lovemaking with this person in your mind, if that is what you want and where you choose to go. Enjoy the pleasurable sensations. Afterward, what happens?

Communicating with Your Ideal Partner

For a few moments, take a psychic stroll with the man or woman of your future. Imagine walking with this person while you engage in conversation. Ask questions in your mind and listen carefully to the answers. Here are a few guidelines, but don't limit yourself to these questions—ask whatever is really important to you.

1. How old is this person? (A general age range is best.)
2. Does he have/want children?
3. Would she prefer to live in the mountains, near the ocean, or in the heart of a large city?
4. What kind of work does he do?
5. What type of temperament does she have? Is she quiet, talkative, assertive, shy, or mysterious?
6. What hobbies or interests does he enjoy?
7. What about political views? Religion (or lack of it)?
8. What's her family like?
9. What friends does he have?
10. What kind of humor does she enjoy?

Now envision the person sitting next to you, ready to respond to your questions. You may hear the answers in your head, receive pictures in your mind, or experience feelings. Whatever impressions you get are okay. Pay attention to your own values and tastes. Remember, this is your creation; it's you who will be involved with this person.

Practice, Practice, Practice

For three days, repeat this process. Your commitment is critical. There's that word *commitment* once again. You don't want to visualize half of the person of your dreams. You must devote 100 percent of your efforts toward your goal. You can't fail when all your energy is focused on making your dream real. The results of your efforts may astonish and will certainly delight you.

As I've said before, thoughts, feelings, and words have energy. Each night, program your mind with the visualization you've created. Seize that golden time right before sleep envelops you to further direct your mind with supportive positive affirmations as well. Through using affirmations, you reinforce your commitment to explore the mind's full potential by drawing upon your own psychic abilities, awakening and empowering them. You establish an environment in which greater opportunities can emerge.

Repeat positive affirmations such as, "I now have the perfect person for me in my life" or "I am now married to the most wonderful person" or "I am so delighted to have this magnificent person in my life." And for those few moments *believe*. Through your openness to believe, you make it possible to receive what you have been visualizing.

It bears repeating: What you believe about yourself *will* be your reality. Nothing happens by accident, big or small. Cause and energy exist behind everything. In the arena of human life, we create the energy and set up the cause with our thinking.

Remember, though, it's your feelings that count the most, not the words. Words can be verbalized or written, but you must have feelings behind them to propel them into action. Approach your visualization with joy and laughter as you give positive messages to your subconscious mind. Generating and releasing positive energy will help attract into your life what and whom you are mentally programming. In the process, your own psychic awareness is expanding and deepening.

The more you use these techniques, the better you'll get. So practice, practice, and then practice some more. Results probably won't happen overnight, but they will happen if you follow these basic steps. We have all heard the expression "if you can see it, you can be it." It's true. Whatever the mind can conceive and believe, it can achieve.

The Final Step

Now comes the most important step in this exhilarating adventure. On the fourth morning, quit thinking all those wonderful thoughts. *You must release the thoughts so that they can become reality.* This is one of the most important lessons, and perhaps the most difficult.

In total confidence, release the thoughts into the universe so that they may return to you in kind. Each time you catch yourself thinking of the man or woman you have mentally created, distract yourself with a different thought. If you wish, use your newly developed visualization skills to attract some other desire into your life, such as prosperity or career success. Release is difficult for many people, but it is essential. I tell my clients it's like filling out a mail-order form. You put in the size, the color, the code number, even make out and sign the check for your purchase, but if you don't send in the form you'll never receive that order.

This is the entire psychic plan, and it is one that only you can develop for yourself. I can't produce it for you. No professional psychic can. A computerized dating matchmaking system can't. You harness and crystallize your own thoughts, emotions, and energies. Have no doubt the person you imagine will come into your life. Just *know*, deep inside. Your belief will allow time to be your ally. When it happens doesn't matter; enjoy the now. Try it! I wish both you and the person you meet joy and peace in the realization of your deepest desires.

CHAPTER RECAP

Practices such as meditation, visualization, and affirmation that enable you to tap in to the subconscious level of your mind, where old patterns are stored, can help you fundamentally revise and re-create yourself according to your vision of what you want to be and to accomplish *now*. By using these techniques, you can expand your psychic powers and attract whatever you want into your life. In just three days, you can lay the foundation and set up the environment for your future happiness. The keys to manifesting your dreams are desire, effort, and belief. But be careful what you ask for. Know what you really want, and then proceed to create it.

CHAPTER 8

Psychic Healing: The Body-Mind-Spirit Connection

"In every community there is work to be done. In every nation there are wounds to heal. In every heart there is the power to do it."
—Marianne Williamson

We have made phenomenal progress in the field of medical science. On the other hand, are we really any healthier? Why is healthcare such a critical, almost paralyzing issue that worries us all? Why do our bodies still get so sick and hurt so much, so often? Why is obesity a virtual epidemic in our nation, occurring in more than a quarter of the adult population and leading to serious illnesses at earlier ages? Why does cancer claim more than half a million lives annually in the United States alone? Why does Alzheimer's affect more than 26 million people worldwide with estimates predicted to soar to more than 106 million by 2050, according to researchers at the Johns Hopkins Bloomberg School of Public Health?

The most sophisticated, high-tech advances in the world don't address the issue of wholeness, that critical balancing of physical, emotional, psychological, and spiritual health. Your emotions and thoughts can—and do—impact your physical health. Negative thinking and unpleasant emotions cause disharmony, which can manifest as illness in the physical body and a general state of dis-ease.

According to a study published in *U.S. News and World Report* in December 2006, "research has linked having a positive attitude to longer life span. Happier people are less likely to suffer heart attacks, strokes, and pain from conditions like rheumatoid arthritis." Yet few of us are truly happy, and our unhappiness has a destabilizing and destructive effect on our health overall.

When we harbor anger toward others or ourselves, or bottle this emotion up, erecting an internal wall to keep anger inside, the consequences are likely to materialize physically, emotionally, and mentally. If negative emotions find no outward expression or recognition, they burrow deep inside the body. Denied, they manifest outwardly as illness. For example, research published in *Cancer Nursing* in 2000 found that "suppressed anger can be a precursor to the development of cancer, and also a factor in its progression after diagnosis."

What Is Psychic Healing?

You've probably heard of psychic healing. In such cases, seemingly miraculous physical transformations take place, without any type of conventional medical intervention. In *The Book of Awakening*, Mark Nepo writes about being healed of brain cancer when a priest placed his hands on Nepo's head and psychically dissolved the tumors. Healing can even happen over long distances, or without the ill person's knowledge. It may occur through practices such as laying on of hands, prayer, or other means. While researching his books *Healing Words* and *Prayer Is Good Medicine*, Larry Dossey, MD, discovered that "more than 130 controlled laboratory studies show that prayer, or a prayer-like state of compassion, empathy and love, can bring about healthful changes."

Healing modalities such as Reiki, biofeedback, hypnotherapy, and homeopathy could also be considered forms of psychic healing because they balance the psyche, adjust life energy, and harmonize the emotions to bring about healing. In fact, all holistic healing is based on the concept that mind and body cannot be separated, and that when a problem exists, both must be addressed if healing is to succeed.

Health Depends on Mind-Body Balance

When we're out of balance, out of harmony, we become ill. The most obvious example—one even conventional medicine recognizes—is how stress diminishes the body's natural resistance ability and impacts the immune system, setting the stage for the onslaught of disease or the worsening of existing medical problems. We've all had the experience of being under pressure at work or in our personal lives, letting ourselves get stressed out, and coming down with a cold or the flu as a result. Our thoughts and feelings are the cause, and discomfort and illness are the effect.

How can negative thinking produce physical imperfections in the body?
Think of negativity as a kind of poison. Thoughts can contaminate your system just as surely as arsenic can. Worry, fear, and anger produce negative energy. So do jealousy, destructive

criticism, and cynicism. When thoughts and memories—either held in the mind or expressed outwardly—are gloomy, unkind, judgmental, or caustic, they prompt adverse reactions within the mind and body, especially if they are harbored over an extended period of time.

Are there ways to get rid of negative energy?

Yes. Negative energy doesn't appear out of the blue. Something fosters it, brings it along, perhaps a thought or a stressful situation. Identify what that something is. Know your enemy—that's the first rule in winning a conflict. Once you have the enemy in sight, then you can plan an attack.

Here are some ways to shift the mind-body balance toward the positive, healthy end of the spectrum:

- Focus completely on the positive things in your life. Count your blessings. Name them. Write them down. Express gratitude for them.
- Daydream about something wonderful that you wish for yourself. Daydream as if the situation has already happened.
- Make a list of positive affirmations that describe conditions as you want them to be.
- Laugh. Buy a joke book or comedy recording, watch a funny movie; do something that will make you laugh at least once a day.
- Do something you enjoy every day, whether it's taking a walk, reading a good book, talking to a friend on the phone, or stroking your pet. While you're engaged in this activity, devote your entire attention to it and take pleasure in it.

- Smile often. Throughout the day, busy yourself and your mind with things that prompt a smile. Smile at everyone you see, and mentally send them healing thoughts.

When you give positive things top priority in your thoughts and your life, you automatically relegate the negative ones to the back burner. They diminish in importance. A positive attitude allows you to cope with stress, grief, loss, and risk. Never forget that positive equals power.

How does psychic healing work?

Psychic healing works through your own physical energy. Physical matter is made up of atoms, which in turn are composed of electrons, protons, and neutrons—all energy. This energy is always in motion. I've discussed how your thoughts and feelings can influence and change what is going on in your physical being. A thought can make you shiver, drool, cringe, or smile.

One crucial ingredient in this formula is to recognize the importance of fostering your own energy. Many caregivers diligently minister to other people, but neglect their own well-being. Don't let your energy get too low. Don't wear yourself out. Carve out a time for meditation. Nourish yourself. Do things you enjoy. Rest and relax. Your own energy must be operating at a high level if you are going to help other people—you can't give someone else something you don't have yourself.

The key is to believe this is possible. To doubt is to set up a roadblock. To believe is to provide a pathway for the power that flows through you. Belief sets things in motion. If you can't believe wholeheartedly, pretend that you do until you finally convince yourself. Proceed as though you believe, and don't let doubt monopolize your thoughts.

SHAKE OFF NEGATIVE ENERGY EXERCISE

Try this breathing exercise to release negative energy. Wear loose-fitting clothes.

1. Sit up straight in a place where you feel comfortable, with your feet flat on the floor and your hands on your knees with palms facing up. The index and middle finger and the thumb of each hand should touch each other, forming a triangle.

2. Close your eyes.

3. Relax by taking several deep, slow breaths. Once you feel you are ready, take a deep breath through the nose and hold it for the count of seven. Release your breath slowly through the mouth and relax. Breathe normally for four or five breaths, and then once again take a deep breath through the nose and hold it for the count of seven. Release the breath, very slowly through the mouth, then relax and breathe normally.

4. Continue this breathing sequence for several minutes, or until you feel your energy shift to a more positive place. Little by little you will feel a greater sense of peacefulness envelop you.

BREATHING TECHNIQUE TO BALANCE ENERGY

Here's a second breathing exercise that can help you establish an energy balance.

1. Sit up straight with your feet flat on the floor and touching.
2. Bring your hands together so your fingertips are touching— thumb to thumb, pinky to pinky, and so forth.
3. Close your eyes and take a deep breath. Exhale slowly. When you've expelled all the air from your lungs, pause there for the count of five before inhaling again. Then breathe normally, in and out easily and slowly, for about four or five breaths until you are once again relaxed.
4. Again, take a deep breath, exhale all the air out of your body, and pause there for a count of five. Repeat this sequence several times. Enjoy feeling increasingly relaxed.
5. When you're ready, open your eyes.

I can't emphasize this enough: We dissipate our precious energy in a thousand ways, most of the time unnecessarily. Worry, fear, resentment, and anger are all major energy drains. Regardless of whether these emotions and thoughts are directed toward others or toward yourself, they consume large amounts of your vital energy. When you waste energy, your psychic awareness and all your mind-body resources suffer.

Changing Your Energy Patterns

By programming your mind for health and harnessing the good energy of your thoughts, you can prompt a remarkable healing process for yourself. Loving, joyful, peaceful thoughts relax your body and promote harmonious conditions; stress, anxiety, and fear, on the other hand, cause tension and turmoil in your body.

You can actually measure the harmful impact of anger and anxiety by checking your body's cortisol levels. Known as the stress hormone, cortisol is released during periods of stress. Studies have shown that laughter reduces cortisol levels and that lowering stress is one of the healthiest things you can do for your body.

Meditation is one of the most effective ways to shift accomplish that. It can help change your thinking and energy patterns. In 1987, the journal *Psychosomatic Medicine* published results of a five-year study of meditation and health that involved thousands of participants. It showed that people over the age of forty who meditated spent almost 70 percent fewer days in the hospital than their peers who didn't meditate; meditators also had nearly three-quarters fewer outpatient visits. Talk about psychic healing!

Can I change my energy patterns? Can I heal myself?

Emphatically, yes! Yes, you can in many cases—through meditation, visualization, and affirmations. I did, and you can, too. Certainly, physical exercise, healthy eating habits, and restraint in tobacco, alcohol, and other drug use are important avenues to pursue. But psychic healing practices can work effectively as well.

In some instances, of course, medication can aid the body's natural healing process—but often that benefit comes at a price. Many drugs and medical treatments produce unwanted side effects that may be almost as unpleasant as the discomfort of the illness itself. We're discovering we can't throw pills at everything. Use the power of thought, meditation, positive affirmations, visualizations, and prayers to activate the body's natural healing process. Listen to your body. Think of yourself as your primary care physician, because you are.

Body Talk

Earlier I mentioned medical intuitives. The term refers to physicians, therapists, or healers who use intuition to diagnose health problems. In some cases, a medical intuitive does a psychic "body scan" to determine what's wrong with a patient, in a manner similar to what an MRI does, except she uses her mind instead of a machine to check the patient's body. The physician employs intuition—her inner vision and feelings, her sixth sense—to tune in to what the ill person's body is trying to communicate.

For example, a person who has trouble speaking up for himself may suffer from throat problems. The medical intuitive might see or sense a lump or other type of blockage in the person's throat. Or, she might notice the patient's throat chakra, an energy center located near the base of the throat, isn't a normal, healthy blue color but instead is distorted or dull.

If someone experiences digestive problems, it could indicate he is having trouble digesting some situation in his life. A person whose hips or knees are crippled with arthritis might psychologically be having difficulty taking the necessary steps to move forward in her life.

What's your body trying to tell you? Consider some of the expressions we use and their related physical conditions. If your neck hurts, think about what is "giving you a pain in the neck." If you have ulcers, what's "eating you up inside"? Have you come down with the flu because you are "sick and tired" of putting up with a situation in your life? Listen to what your body is saying— and what you're saying about your body.

Affirmations and Healing

As discussed previously, an affirmation is a positive statement that you say aloud or think to yourself. You give your subconscious mind a command when you create and repeat an affirmation—in this case, to heal yourself. Once you have stepped forward and committed to reaching a goal, and once you have made daily affirmations part of your mission, you will begin to perceive the results. You will feel the energy flowing through your entire body—muscles, cells, organs, and bones. You will feel the power, the exhilaration, and an overwhelming sense of appreciation.

Are affirmations a type of psychic healing?

Absolutely. They help to heal your psyche, and in so doing, they also help to heal your body. Earlier, I wrote about my own experiences with debilitating back problems and how I healed myself through visualization and affirmation. You can do the same thing. Tell your body to be healthy, and expect health to come. Concentrate on areas that have been hurting and visualize these areas becoming well. Remember to affirm and visualize yourself in a state of perfect health and wholeness—don't focus on the ailment, focus on the end result you desire.

Make a list of positive affirmations. Here are some statements you could use:

- "I am completely healthy in body, mind, and spirit."
- "My body is balanced and in perfect harmony with the universe."
- "My mind and body are perfectly healthy, and functioning optimally."

Record yourself speaking your positive affirmations aloud, if you like. You can use several related affirmations, like those above, or repeat the same one over and over. You can create a narrative such as, "I am getting stronger every day. I am doing what is right for my body and my life." The statement(s) you choose can be long or short, but record your voice stating your affirmation(s) again and again for at least fifteen to twenty minutes. Play the recording back while you are practicing your breathing exercises, or while you are doing something solitary, such as walking (with headphones) or taking a bath at night.

Activating the Healing Process

Life energy flows through you and every living creature. It's yours to use. You are energy. In Chinese medicine, this life force is called chi or qi (pronounced chee). Acupuncturists focus on removing blockages that can obstruct the way chi flows through your body and that ultimately produce illness. These blockages may be caused by stress, emotional trauma, or a host of other conditions. By reestablishing energetic harmony, acupuncture (and its less invasive form known as acupressure) facilitates the smooth flow of chi and promotes healing. Other holistic healing methods use the same concept—breaking down energy blockages to restore balance and well-being. Massage and reflexology (rubbing specific points on the feet that correlate with the various parts of the body) are two safe and easy techniques you can do yourself to facilitate the smooth flow of energy through your own body or someone else's.

Your mind and body are in constant communication. You may not be paying attention to your thoughts and feelings, but your body is, your subconscious mind is, and your intuition is. Remember what I said about positive thinking? One of the most famous examples of activating the natural healing process by changing thought patterns is that of Norman Cousins, a former magazine editor for the *Saturday Review* who was diagnosed with autoimmune disease. He supposed that positive emotions could aid in his recovery, and set about healing himself through laugh therapy. Cousins designed a program for himself that involved watching lots of humorous movies and TV programs. And it worked. His disease went into remission. His story was published in the *New England Journal of Medicine* and in his bestselling book *Anatomy of an Illness: A Patient's Perspective*.

The Healing Power of Prayer

Don't be afraid to ask others to pray for you. If that request does not fit your personal life philosophy, ask something like, "Please send good thoughts my way" or "Think about me as I go through this difficulty."

Can you use psychic healing to help other people?

Healing others? Does that sound like hocus-pocus to you? Just as I have suggested you ask others to send positive thoughts and/or prayers your way, so, too, can you reciprocate. Visualize your ill friend as being pain free and healthy. Don't focus on her ailment. If you are in an exercise group, a meditation group, or even a bunch-for-lunch group, suggest to others that all of you send positive energy to each other, as well as to people you know who are suffering with ills.

Dr. Larry Dossey, author of *Prayer Is Good Medicine*, became intrigued by the idea that prayer could aid the healing process when he read about a 1988 study of cardiac patients who, after being prayed for without their knowledge, got better at a surprising rate. Many spiritual organizations host prayer groups and pray for people they don't know as well as for those in their immediate circle. One of the oldest prayer groups in the United States is the Unity School of Christianity's Silent Unity group, based in Unity Village, Missouri. Begun more than a hundred years ago, the organization has hundreds of workers who handle the thousands of prayer requests that flow in constantly. Every request is blessed by the volunteer who receives it. Members of Silent Unity pray together twice each morning. Every half hour throughout the day, workers pray alone, one after the other, in the Prayer Vigil Chapel, keeping the vigil going continuously.

Whether you call it prayer or simply sending good thoughts to someone who's ailing, the positive energy you generate will have a beneficial effect on the recipient—and on you as well.

CHAPTER RECAP

You have the power to heal yourself and others by utilizing your psychic ability. Many forms of holistic healing, including laying on of hands, prayer, biofeedback, and hypnotherapy, can be considered psychic healing modalities. They treat both *psyche* (mind) and *soma* (body), and bring them into harmony. In fact, all holistic healing practices address both the mind and the body, in order to establish balance and well-being.

Not only can you use your psychic powers to improve your own health, you can send healing energy to other people. Stress, anger, and negative thinking drain your natural vitality, whereas positive thinking and happiness bolster your immune system and reinforce your innate health. Be aware of how your thoughts and emotions affect your well-being, and use this psychic power wisely.

CHAPTER 9

Psychometry: Picking Up and Interpreting Vibes

"Intuition isn't the enemy, but the ally, of reason."

—John Kord Lagema

Psychometry is the intuitive art of picking up and interpreting information by holding or touching objects. The word psychometry is derived from two Greek words, *psyche*, meaning the soul, and *merton*, meaning to measure. When given an object to hold, psychics can sense characteristic qualities or energies emanating from that object—what we might call "vibes"—that enable them to zero in on past, present, and future events associated with the person who handled, used, or wore the object.

When I work with police to solve missing persons cases and homicides, I use this method to connect with the subject of the investigation. As soon as I touch the object that belonged to the person being sought, I start receiving psychic impressions. I see visions as if I were looking through the eyes of the other person—sometimes entire scenes, sometimes just quick or disjointed glimpses. I tune in to the emotions of that person. I may experience pain, confusion, fear, distress, or other sensations. In some cases, I get an "aha" feeling and I just *know* what happened.

The reason a psychic can pick up this type of information from personal objects is that they absorb the vibration patterns of the people who carried, wore, or used them. These vibrations create an energy memory that reflects the circumstances surrounding the object's owner. The energy memory can vary from weak to strong, depending on the owner's personality.

For a psychic, holding an object that belonged to another person is like dialing her personal number or frequency. The psychic can tune in to the person's energy and sense what's going on in her life, what she's feeling, emitting, and attracting. In some ways, it's a little like sitting in someone else's chair or wearing another person's coat. Have you ever accidentally taken the wrong coat or hat off a rack and, though it may look like yours, it didn't quite feel like yours? You could sense someone else's energy clinging to it. Amplify this response and you will have an inkling of how it feels to tune in psychically to someone else's energy vibrations.

Developing Psychometric Skills

Becoming adept at the art of psychometry requires proper preparation. Again, I'm talking about developing your psychic awareness. The first step is to start paying attention to the world and the people around you. If you don't have the ability to observe closely, psychometry will be difficult for you. If you can't see the material world sharply, you won't be able to see energies in the psychic world very well, either.

In the intuitive realm, sights, smells, sounds, emotions, and so on are more subtle and less clearly defined than in the objective, physical world. Therefore, people who have trained themselves to be sensitive to the material world around them (or who possess a naturally heightened awareness) are more likely to be able to perceive psychometric vibrations. You could relate it to wine tasting. A highly skilled sommelier will be able to detect very subtle qualities in the wine he tastes that tell him about the region where the grapes were grown, how the wine was processed, and so on, whereas someone who has little interest in wine might miss all these intricacies entirely.

You'd be surprised how much we miss by focusing on some things while completely blocking out others. For instance, if you're taking a walk with a friend and talking about what you plan to do later in the day, you probably won't notice your surroundings in as much detail as you might if you were walking alone and really paying attention to your environment. The best psychics are objective, attentive, and have trained their senses to work at highly acute levels. To acquire this level of skill, you need to fine-tune your senses. The more aware you are of what's going on around you, the greater success you will have sensing and interpreting the impressions and energy transmitted by objects with which you come in contact.

Observation Techniques to Train Your Psychic Perception

Try practicing some simple observation techniques in order to sharpen your awareness. Artists often see details other people miss, partly because they've trained themselves to pay close attention to colors, shadows, and light. The exercises presented here train your mind to pay attention and to notice things you may have ignored before. By increasing your ability to observe physical things, you'll simultaneously hone your skill at perceiving nonphysical things, such as auras.

OBSERVING AND REMEMBERING EVERYDAY OBJECTS

Ask a friend or family member to place twelve everyday items on a tray, and then hand the tray to you. Observe the tray for sixty seconds. Then turn your back on it and try to recall all twelve items. How many did you remember? Try this again with different objects. You may discover you are able to remember certain types of things better than others, or that you can recall colors better than shapes (or vice versa).

NOTICING MORE OF THE WORLD AROUND YOU

Look around your workspace or home and try to find things you have never noticed before. On the way to and from work or the grocery store, see how many "new" things you observe. Get into the habit of paying attention to what's happening around you, instead of moving automatically from moment to moment, hour to hour, and place to place like a zombie. Just as there is much we don't know, likewise, there is much of which we're unaware—and often the two are related. In some instances, what seems to be second sight is actually utilizing your ordinary sight more intently.

SHARPEN ALL YOUR SENSES

The first step to developing extrasensory perception is expanding your ordinary sensory perception. Look closely at your surroundings.

1. Zero in on a piece of furniture. Observe its lines, scratches, hues, construction details. You may have eaten dinner on a table for years, yet never really noticed the pattern formed by the wood's grain or the way the apron and legs are joined. Observe a plant. Pay attention to the color variations in its leaves, the way the flower petals come together in the center, and the configuration of the stem.

2. Close your eyes and pay attention to the different sounds around you. Name them, count them, imitate them. Listen to the changes in the velocity of the wind and the sounds the leaves in the trees make as the wind ruffles them. When you hear a bird sing, try to sense how the bird might be feeling or what he might be trying to express. Put an instrumental CD on your sound system and see if you can distinguish the different musical instruments playing.

3. Focus on smells. Aromas instantly trigger the limbic system, the part of the brain associated with memory and emotions. That's why smells can bring back scenes from your past, such as baking cookies with Grandma when you were a child. Practice smelling various things in your home that you might not ordinarily sniff—a book, a glove, a cardboard box, a stone—and see what you notice. Go to a perfume store and experiment with smelling new scents.

4. When you're eating, go slowly and try to notice the subtle flavors in your food. Pay attention to how and where your tongue picks up tastes—on the tip? The back of the tongue? The sides? Eat a sauce, casserole, or soup with many different flavors and spices in it, and try to determine as many ingredients as possible.

5. Notice how different things feel when you touch them. Experiment with stroking various types of fabrics such as velvet, silk, corduroy, linen, wool, cashmere. Observe the texture, the weave of the cloth, and the nap.

Practice these sensory exercises indoors and outdoors. You can use this technique anywhere, anytime: at work, at play, in your garden, on a beach, riding a bus, or on the subway. You'll soon find endless ways to sharpen your awareness and have fun in the process.

People Watching

In my work with police, I've had to develop my ability to notice details in people's faces, physical features, gestures, and clothing in order to provide accurate descriptions of perpetrators and victims. You, too, can strengthen your perceptual capabilities by people watching. Try observing people when you're at airports, restaurants, and sporting events. Pay attention to small details, not just the obvious things. What's unique or distinctive about someone?

I've often worked with police sketch artists to create portraits that can be used to help identify and locate suspects. As I hold an object that belonged to a victim, I get psychic visions of the person(s) who was in the victim's presence at the time the event occurred. I have to pay close attention to the eyes, nose, mouth, and other features of anyone the victim may have encountered in order to be able to convey what I've witnessed to a sketch artist.

You can practice describing the features of people you see on television (or on the Internet). Think about how you would convey those eyes or that nose to an artist. How about the mouth and the shape of the face? When the news is on television, describe the newscaster to yourself. Pretend you're giving this information to an artist. Later, when you're not looking at the television, try putting your impressions into a drawing. You don't have to be an artist yourself—this exercise is simply to sharpen your observation and memory skills. Just do the best you can.

The following list includes facial features an artist would use to make a composite sketch of a face. This list shows you what you need to be aware of when describing the face. You won't be able to capture them all, of course. However, you can have fun and test yourself by putting yourself in the shoes of an artist who's trying to do a composite from scratch.

Eyes
- Color
- Bulging eyes (coming forward)
- Squinting eyes
- Deep-set eyes
- Close-set eyes
- Wide-set eyes
- Open eyes
- Round or oval-shaped eyes
- Heavy (droopy, sleepy) eyelids
- Thick, thin, bushy, or manicured eyebrows
- Eyebrow color
- Space between eyes and eyebrows

Nose

- Average
- Long
- Short
- Wide
- Narrow
- Crooked or bent
- Large tip or small
- Orientation of the tip of the nose (pointing up, down, or level with the nostrils)
- Visibility of nostrils
- Shape of nostrils

Mouth

- Large
- Small
- Shape of upper lip
- Shape of lower lip
- Mountain on top of lips (peaks, round)
- Lines around mouth
- Distance between mouth and nose
- Size of teeth
- Color of teeth
- Straight teeth or crooked
- Missing teeth

Head Shape

- Round
- Oval
- Square
- Triangular
- Long
- Irregular

Cheeks

- Prominent (high cheekbones)
- Not prominent (flattish cheekbones)
- Sunken cheeks
- Sagging
- Jowly
- Puffy/plump
- Dimples or lines

Chin

- Average
- Jutting (pushed out)
- Pointed
- Receding (pushed in)
- Square
- Double chin
- Cleft
- Short
- Long

Forehead

- Average
- High
- Low
- Smooth (unwrinkled)
- Furrowed

Ears

- Average
- Protruding
- Close-set
- Large
- Small
- Long earlobes
- Short earlobes
- Earrings

Hair

- Color
- Straight
- Wavy/curly
- Balding/receding
- Length
- Style (bob, pixie, ponytail, dreadlocks)

Facial Hair

- None
- Mustache or beard
- Mustache shape and thickness
- Beard, full or goatee
- Color of facial hair

Other Identifiers

- Glasses (shape, color)
- Scars (acne scars, cuts, burns, other)
- Marks (moles, birthmarks, freckles, warts, et cetera)
- Texture of skin (coarse, rough-looking, acne, smooth, weathered)
- Tattoos on face or body
- Lines or wrinkles indicating age
- Jewelry

As I explained earlier, training yourself to more accurately observe the physical world strengthens not only your everyday perceptual abilities, it also improves your second sight and intuitive recall. Clairvoyance, which literally means clear seeing or seeing something with your inner sight rather than your physical eyes, can be enhanced by practicing this technique, too.

As you develop your psychic power, you may discover that images come to you regularly, and these may include images of people (either people you've known or people you have never met). For instance, you might get a vision of someone you will meet in the future and it could be important to remember the image you receive, so you'll recognize that person later. But unless you've mastered the art of visual recognition, you might miss out on valuable information that's being conveyed to you.

Once when I was trying to describe a client's husband, I thought the man I saw in my psychic vision was someone I knew. I believed I was on the wrong track—my logical mind stepped in, and this stopped the flow of my impressions. The next time I tried it, I didn't attempt to pigeonhole the man in my vision; I simply described his features as they appeared to me. What I described perfectly matched my client's beloved.

Even though the above exercise centers on distinguishing and describing facial features, the same skills of observation can be applied in countless ways. Honing your ability to observe, discern, and remember what you perceive can prove valuable in both psychic activity and everyday life. When we get to Chapter 13 on dreams, you'll see how this technique can also help you remember your dreams in greater detail and understand what they're trying to tell you.

Psychometry Exercises

To practice psychometry, you'll need objects to hold. Metal items are ideal. So are pieces of jewelry, so long as only one person has worn them. I once held a ring that belonged to a grandmother, but had also been worn by her daughter and granddaughter. Consequently, I saw images and got impressions of all three generations of women. Dense objects that endure for many years without degrading—metal and gemstones in particular—retain the energy or vibrational imprint of their owners for a very long time, and therefore effectively convey information to a psychic.

Fabric, by contrast, doesn't work as well because it has often been washed and cleansed of the person's energy.

In private sessions, I prefer to hold a small piece of the individual's hair. Hair is highly personal and unique, imbued with a great deal of energy. Another good object is a letter or card from the person. Handwritten ones especially embody vibrations because the writer imparts energy, both from physical contact with the paper and from the emotion involved in composing the letter or card.

The goal of psychometry is to be able to pick up and interpret the energy fields of a person, object, or photograph. Remember, you want to observe, not react or use your logical mind. As you hold an object, you are simply gathering information intuitively, assimilating impressions, and tuning in to sensations. Don't attempt to analyze or categorize them.

It can be tempting to attempt to identify or name something you see with your inner sight. Once when I was trying to describe the area surrounding a suspect's home, I saw what looked like my own backyard. Because the fence and trees in my yard were similar to the suspect's, my logical mind jumped to conclusions. Of course, it wasn't my own yard I saw in my vision, and when I simply described the features I observed, they matched those in the suspect's yard. Even with the mundane things you see psychically, don't analyze and name them; just describe them. If, for instance, you see a Christmas tree, don't say, "I see a Christmas tree," just describe it. This is the rational mind jumping in to try to define and pin down your vision, which can interfere with the flow of psychic information because your rational mind has already drawn conclusions. It's better to simply let your inner sight observe as many details as possible, in a detached, objective manner.

In the beginning, while you are still a novice, stay with impressions and feelings that relate to the present or past. Don't attempt to see into a person's future. That's an area you cannot verify or confirm, so you can't test your accuracy. When you have developed your skill, you can venture into an individual's future with more awareness and confidence.

PICKING UP A STRANGER'S VIBES

Ask a friend or family member to select an item that belongs to someone you don't know, such as a ring. It is very important that you don't know the person to whom the object belongs. Your intent is to psychometrize, or, in other words, to psychically describe the owner. Hold the ring and close your eyes.

Experiment by holding the ring in one hand, and then the other. Stroke the ring gently and tell your mind you want to see the person to whom the ring belongs. You may see a full face, but you may not. It's not unusual to get bits and pieces of a person's features, perhaps an eye or the shape of the face. That's how I generally perceive a person when I'm using psychometry. Impressions may flash very quickly into your mind and it can be hard to take them all in. Some psychics talk rapidly because they are receiving impressions so quickly. This is one of the reasons you need to train your mind to observe and remember details, using the exercises presented earlier in this chapter.

Record or write down what you see and what you feel. You may not see anything, but perhaps you'll receive some feelings. If that's the case, continue talking about what you're feeling (if you are with another person who is writing down what you say, or if you are recording your session). Remember, you're looking for impressions that can be verified and for which you can provide feedback. Express whatever comes into your mind. Nothing may feel very certain in the beginning because the visions or feelings are so subtle. Don't get rattled. Go with the flow. Persevere.

When you've finished, verify your impressions about the owner of the ring with your friend or relative who actually knows the owner. How accurate were you? Did you see visions, receive feelings, or both? Did you get some clear impressions and some vague ones? Were some of the vague ones in the ballpark, even if they weren't exact? For example, did you sense the owner as being warm, and it turned out he presently happens to be vacationing in Mexico? Keep a record of your hits. With practice, your psychometry skills will most likely improve. Your journey of psychic awareness is becoming more authentic, more fulfilling, and more exciting.

READING LETTERS WITH PSYCHOMETRY

Collect a few handwritten letters to initiate a practice session. These should be letters from someone you know—a friend or relative, for example—or perhaps a signature on a Christmas card or birthday message. I am leery of using unverifiable letters; you might want to be certain of the relationship between the letter writer and the recipient ahead of time.

1. Place the letters or cards in identical envelopes so you cannot differentiate one from the other.
2. Mix them up, so you don't know which envelope contains which letter/card, and then number the envelopes.
3. Spread them out on a table or other surface.
4. Once you have the envelopes arranged, sit in a comfortable chair and relax yourself as much as possible. Being tense or nervous will block your ability to sense subtle energies.

You may wish to meditate in advance to help remove any tension or distractions.

5. Know your objectives. Consider describing the writer of the letter or card and his emotional state or physical characteristics. Perhaps you'd like to see if you can intuitively sense the era or place where the letter was written.

6. Write a few questions on a piece of paper and either record your answers or write them down. Ask the same questions for each envelope. Be confident. In the beginning, it's okay to just ramble on about what you perceive, what you sense, and what your developing psychic awareness is conveying to you. Later on, when you become more adept, you can ask your mind specific questions. Keep notes on your impressions from each individual letter/card.

7. When you've finished tuning in to all the letters, open the envelopes and take out the letters. Peruse them and compare what you read to the notes you've taken or the statements you've made on the recording.

How accurate were you? Could you sense anything about the people who wrote the letters? Sex, age, nationality, temperament, appearance? How about the recipients? If you used some letters from people you knew and some from people you didn't know, could you tell the difference between the energy of friends/ relatives and that of complete strangers? Were you able to pick up vibes about the writers' emotional states or the content of the letters? Did you have any near-misses in which you sensed something close, even though your interpretation wasn't exact? For instance, did you get an impression of fear and it turned out the letter was written by a soldier during wartime?

GROUP PSYCHOMETRY EXERCISE

Do this exercise with several friends and/or family members. You'll need three or four people at least.

1. Ask each person to place a key (car, house, place of business) that belongs to him or her in an envelope. If it's possible that people won't be able to recognize their own keys, ask each one to also put in the envelope a slip of paper with his/her name written on it. Then seal the envelopes.

2. Put all the envelopes in a basket and mix them up, so it's impossible to tell which envelope contains which key. Pass the basket around and ask each person to draw an envelope from it.

3. Take a few moments to tune in to the keys within the envelopes. Don't handle the envelopes in such a way that you could determine logically what's inside by feel.

4. Each person then writes down whatever he or she senses about the key's owner—car, house, workplace, appearance, emotions, identifying characteristics, health issues, occupation, and so on. Even if it seems illogical, meaningless, or silly, write it down anyway. You might pick up something you couldn't possibly have known with your rational mind. Perhaps you'll get an image of red lace and it turns out the key's owner is wearing red lace underwear.

5. It's always interesting when someone unknowingly gets his or her own key. I tell my students not to be startled if they see their bedrooms or kitchens—just describe it, don't identify it.

6. When everyone has finished, open the envelopes. Read your impressions. Describe how you arrived at these responses. How accurate were you? How accurate were the other people in your group?

PSYCHICALLY VIEWING PHOTOGRAPHS

When I work with police to help them solve crimes, I'm sometimes asked to pick a suspect from a group of photos without actually viewing the photographs. It's a little like choosing a suspect from a police lineup, but with your eyes closed. This exercise tests your ability to elicit psychic clues from photographs without seeing the photos themselves. You can do this exercise alone or with other people.

1. Collect about a dozen photographs. All photos should be the same size and shape. They may depict people, landscapes, animals, buildings, plants, or anything else. They may show people or places you know, or ones with which you have no obvious knowledge or connection.
2. Shuffle the photos so you don't know which is which. Then lay them out face down on a table or other surface.
3. After taking a few moments to calm and center yourself, hold your hand with the palm facing down over each photo individually.
4. Write down whatever impressions you pick up—visions, emotions, or other sensations.
5. When you feel you've gleaned everything you can, move on to the next photograph and do the same thing.
6. Continue in this manner until you've psychically examined every photograph and noted your reactions to it.

7. Then turn the photos face up. Compare the photos with what you've written.

How accurate were you? What sort of impressions did you get? Visual? Sensory? Emotional? Were you on target in some cases, but not even in the ballpark with others? Did you get close in some instances? For example, if a photo showed a cat, did you sense fur? If you're allergic to cats, did your nose tickle or your eyes itch?

If you are practicing this exercise with other people, shuffle the photos again—or use different pictures—and let the next person have a go at it. When everyone has had a chance, compare your results. Were there any similar responses? Did some people react visually whereas others got emotional impressions? Did you have more success identifying photos of people/places you know than with those you don't know?

With practice, you'll be able to pick up a person's energy from any object, and interpret that energy to a greater or lesser degree. Some objects may belong to highly charged, emotional people. If you pick up strong emotions, be certain only to observe and not absorb the vibrations. You do not want to let this energy affect you emotionally or physically.

Before you begin a psychometry session, you can envision yourself completely surrounded by a ball of pure white light that protects you from taking on the energies and emotions of the person to whom the object belongs. Another way to stay detached is to tell yourself that you are flying above the scene and simply observing it with a bird's-eye view. You are not a participant in whatever you see.

I generally try to use the latter technique when I'm remotely viewing a crime scene in my police work. Because many of the cases I get involved with include violence and suffering—and police always want me to describe how a victim was murdered—I prefer to fly above the scenario and report what I observe, instead of feeling what the victim experienced. Tell yourself in advance that you will remain calm, you will not feel any anxiety or pain, and that you will merely see and describe whatever you witness. You might ask a friend or relative to work with you and repeat this to you if you start picking up feelings that seem troubling to you.

A Few Ethical Guidelines and Precautions

Should you see or feel something terrible happening to an individual whose object you are psychometrizing, remain calm and be discreet. Communicate these impressions carefully, without a lot of drama. Should you ever see death, warn the person to be careful or suggest a medical checkup. Avoid telling someone you see his or her death, or the death of someone close. This information could be devastating—and you could be wrong.

Once the flow stops and the visions and feelings are no longer there, mentally prepare yourself to disconnect from the object. After releasing the object, shake your hands vigorously and physically wash them when you've finished. This is a way of separating yourself from the energy of the session. If you wish, you can say a prayer or mantra that signifies you are concluding and are now ready to move back into your ordinary life.

Attached to every profession and avocation are guidelines, strictures, conventions, practical dos and don'ts. The same is true when you deal in psychic matters. Here are some tips I've discovered through my own experience and found useful:

- Be careful about volunteering your talent freely. Some people may take advantage of you. Or they may not take you seriously if you provide information too readily or indiscriminately.
- Respect other people's privacy. Don't take objects and do psychometry readings without a person's permission. I can assure you the people involved won't appreciate it. Psychic advice, like any advice, is not usually welcomed if unsolicited. If people want to know something, they'll ask. If they believe you've intruded into a private area—or one they aren't ready to deal with just yet—they may become defensive or annoyed, even if your perceptions are accurate.
- Be honest, but tactful. If you feel confident that what you've intuited is accurate, share what you've seen or sensed. But err on the side of caution. Explain that although you observed something, your interpretation of it may not be correct. *No one is right 100 percent of the time.* It's also possible that conditions could change in the future, and it's wise to mention this. However, you don't want lie to a person who's seeking your help, nor do you want to conceal information or try to put a nice face on an unpleasant situation, even if you think it's in her best interest. You'll only confuse her and undermine your own credibility.
- Be discreet. Respect people's privacy and don't share what you learn in a session with anybody else. A psychic consultation is the equivalent of one with a medical doctor, psychiatrist, or lawyer: any information you receive is confidential.

Outside of these few precautions, don't hesitate to experiment freely. With practice, you can train your psychic response and fine-tune it. You'll soon familiarize yourself with your own unique impressions and what they indicate.

CHAPTER RECAP

Psychometry is the intuitive art of picking up and interpreting information by holding or touching objects. You can sense many things about a person, his environment, circumstances, emotions, health, and so on by tuning in to the energies that remain on an item he used, carried, or wore. These energies are a bit like psychic fingerprints, or scents left behind that dogs can smell.

Some people see visions when employing psychometry, whereas others experience emotions or other sensations. As with other psychic skills, you can teach yourself to become adept at reading people and events through the art of psychometry. Expanding your ability to observe the physical world around you can help you to also perceive the nonphysical world more clearly. Although trained psychics can often intuit a person's past, present, or future simply by touching a personal object, it's usually best in the beginning to stick with present or past information that you can verify.

CHAPTER 10

Remote Viewing: Long-Distance Intuitive Seeing

"Intuition is the supra-logic that cuts out all the routine processes of thought and leaps straight from the problem to the answer."

—Robert Graves

In the early 1970s, the U.S. Central Intelligence Agency and the Pentagon launched a psychic research project at the prestigious Stanford Research Institute (SRI) in Menlo Park, California, directed by H. E. Puthoff. The CIA wanted to determine if remote viewing and other forms of psychic phenomena offered possibilities for intelligence gathering for the purpose of national security.

Ingo Swann, a New York psychic and artist whom I met at a parapsychology conference at the Higgins Center in Hillsdale, New Jersey, was instrumental in creating the Stanford research program. He coined the term "remote viewing" as an alternative to the more general term "clairvoyance," which means seeing things beyond the range of normal visual capabilities. The SRI defined this particular type of psychic activity as "the acquisition and description, by mental means, of information blocked from ordinary perception by distance, shielding, or time." In other words, using your psychic sight to see something far away in terms of time or distance that you couldn't possibly see with your ordinary vision.

Researchers enlisted psychic individuals whom they considered extremely accurate in describing distant locations. They also felt it might be possible to teach people to perform remote viewing, and began training selected noncommissioned military soldiers and officers in the military to become psychic spies. Their job was to view persons and places, and to gather intelligence information on foreign individuals, much as conventional spies do—except in this case the only investigative tool was their psychic ability.

You can tap your own psychic vision the way these early remote viewers did. Although you probably won't be using your second sight to spy for the CIA, you might choose to remote view a potential vacation spot before booking a reservation or get a feel for a workplace situation before you accept a job offer.

Seeing Beyond the Limits of Time and Space

Do you want to travel to other solar systems? Would you like to visit the past or future? You can, by using the psychic skill of remote viewing. Just as the pioneering psychics in the SRI program mentally journeyed to the Soviet Union and other countries during the Cold War era, you can travel mentally to any place or any time period you'd like to visit.

In 2010, I had an opportunity to explore remote viewing techniques with Alexis Champion, PhD, noted French author, researcher, and president of IRIS Intuition Consulting, a non-profit organization he founded to use remote viewing to assist individuals, companies, and police. During our session together, he gave me several sets of three numbers. Each set was a code that represented a "target" (in this case, a place on the globe and an event). Dr. Champion asked me to tune in to the site to which each number series corresponded. I felt myself flying above the landscape, describing places I saw below.

After about twenty minutes he gave me a new set of target numbers and I quickly felt the earth shifting below my feet, buildings falling on me, and then water rushing toward me. I described it as both a manmade and natural disaster. It turned out the number code referenced the Vajont Dam about 100 kilometers north of Venice, Italy. In 1963, heavy rains displaced huge volumes of water over the dam and caused a landslide that killed 2,000 people.

Dr. Champion then tested me to see if I could remotely view future events as well as past ones. He gave me another set of numbers for another target and asked me to describe it. He had pictures that represented the outcome of the event (which he didn't tell me about), a basketball game between the Atlanta Hawks and the Minnesota Timberwolves that was in progress as we spoke. He asked me to see the picture that would tell the outcome of the event—each picture represented a team. I described the photo that represented the Hawks winning, which they did, 111 to 105. After our practice sessions, Dr. Champion invited me to join their team.

If you think you'd like to try remote viewing, the following exercises will help you train your mind to see beyond your ordinary range of vision. Who knows? You may even learn to predict ball games, elections, upcoming disasters, and more.

WHAT'S IN THE BOX?

This exercise helps you develop your clairvoyant skills and expand your second sight so you can begin to see things you couldn't ordinarily see. Ask a friend or helper to select an object and place it in a box, making certain that you cannot see the object and don't know what it is. Then close your eyes and attempt to mentally see inside the box. Relax and allow your clairvoyant abilities to come to the fore. Become receptive to impressions, feelings, and visions—just let them come.

Draw or write down any impressions you get of what is inside the box. You might see or sense a color or shape, or perhaps something related to the object's use. For instance, if a hairbrush is inside the box, you might get an impression of hair. Maybe you'll sense the material from which the object is made. Your sketch or written description does not need to be detailed or specific—don't judge yourself or analyze your impressions.

If you don't feel inclined to draw or write something down, use your psychic awareness to look ahead into the near future. Imagine yourself opening the box and holding the object in your hand. Describe the object and your experience. Relate your impressions aloud to your friend, or have a mental conversation with yourself. Bring all of your senses into the experience. If you aren't getting any impressions, your helper could ask you questions as prompts: Do any shapes emerge in your mind? How about colors? How do you feel emotionally about the object? Is it a single object or does it have different parts?

After you are satisfied that you have completed this process and finished gathering all the information you can about the object, open the box and take out the object inside. Did you accurately describe details of the object itself? Or were your impressions sidetracked by miscellaneous thoughts or other distractions?

Did you originally have any strikingly correct images that for some reason—perhaps lack of confidence or second-guessing yourself—you did not describe or draw?

As with all skills, the more you practice this and other exercises designed to train your clairvoyance, the more confident and capable you'll become.

SCAN THE GLOBE PSYCHICALLY

This exercise is based on a technique from the SCANATE project that the Stanford Research Institute used with early remote viewers. The technique involves seeing a place on earth using only your remote-viewing ability. It should be a place you don't know anything about consciously. You can either work solo or with a friend/assistant for this exercise.

Meditate, relax, and get yourself in your psychic mode. Then ask your friend to select a place anywhere in the world and tell you only its coordinates for latitude and longitude. (If you are working alone, simply pick latitude and longitude coordinates yourself at random.) You should not know the name of the target you are about to visit psychically. Here are a few possibilities:

- Latitude 28 58' N, longitude 86 56' E
- Latitude 36 06' N, longitude 109 21' W
- Latitude 60 08' S, longitude 146 40' W

Close your eyes and allow impressions to come to you of the target you've chosen to view. Tell yourself you will see this target clearly. Use your intuition to sense what the target looks and feels like. Do you see mountains? Bodies of water? What sort of vegetation exists? Are there any buildings? What kind? Is it hot,

154 THE PRACTICAL PSYCHIC

cold, or temperate? Rainy or dry? Do you notice any people or animals? Describe them. If you are too high up in the sky to see clearly, can you mentally lower yourself?

Spend as long as you like remotely viewing this place you've never actually seen with your physical eyes. Note sounds, smells, shapes, colors, and any feelings you get from this place. If you like, you can write down or record your descriptions of this place.

When you are ready, open your eyes and either check a map or go to the Internet and input these coordinates to see how well you have done. You can use Google Earth to get a bird's-eye view of the area.

Maybe you described this place as clearly as if you were a native. Maybe you were way off base. Do not be discouraged. Keep trying. Practice, practice, and practice some more. You'll soon notice your remote viewing skills improving.

Psychic Anthropology

Although it may sound a bit far-fetched to most people, you can apply your remote-viewing skills to see into the unknown territory of the past or future, just as you psychically explored foreign geographic locations in the previous exercises. Basically, the same principles exist. You direct your psychic awareness to see beyond the limitations of time and space, which we normally allow to restrict us. You erase the socially accepted boundaries that only acknowledge the here and now.

Because the psychic realm isn't physical, it isn't governed by the same rules as our ordinary, earthbound reality. In your mind, you can use your remote viewing skills to go anywhere and experience anything you choose—in the present world or in another time period. Once you dispense with the dictates of the physical world and rational thinking, you can even project yourself into other universes.

In the *Journal of Scientific Exploration*, H. E. Puthoff reported that during the Stanford Research Institute studies psychic Ingo Swann remotely viewed Jupiter. Swann saw a ring around the planet, which caused him to think he'd mistakenly viewed Saturn instead. It wasn't until NASA later did an exploratory satellite "flyby" and photographed Jupiter that scientists realized Jupiter does, in fact, have a ring.

One of the reasons for developing your remote viewing abilities is to provide information to the world that the logical mind and scientific tools can't detect. Think what a marvelous boon this skill would be for anthropologists, archeologists, historians, and others who wish to learn more about previous cultures. And how about for scientists who search for knowledge about extraterrestrial life and the existence of worlds beyond our own?

VISIONS OF THE PAST

I met with Dr. David Jones, a professor of anthropology at the University of Central Florida, in his office, which was full of old bones like those you might see in a museum. Dr. Jones was interested in exploring the practical applications of extrasensory perception (ESP). He sought to answer a very specific question: Could people who profess to have psychic ability touch archeological artifacts and the physical remains of ancient people and convey information about the objects that could not be obtained in ordinary ways?

I reached across his desk and picked up an ancient human jawbone from its foam-lined box. Stroking the relic thoughtfully, I asked, "David, why is he in a hole with a bunch of other people?"

Although I didn't know it at the time, the fossilized mandible was that of an adult Indian man who had been buried in a mass grave east of the Great Lakes more than a thousand years ago.

David asked me, "What kind of weather do you feel he experienced?"

I closed my eyes and answered, "He didn't like the cold. There was snow. Cold winters and short summers."

"Noreen, where does this bone come from? Who is it?"

I opened my eyes and casually remarked, "Oh, he's an old Indian man from up north somewhere."

"How do you think he died?" David asked, putting the bone back in its box.

"He didn't die from old age or sickness. He was hit in the head and killed. He didn't have a chance."

In fact, the man's cranium, which was being packed in a separate container in the archeology laboratory, indicated that his death had been caused by a crushing blow to the left side of the head.

I continued working with David for six years. The data he collected from me and three other psychics was published in his book *Visions in Time: Experiments in Psychic Archeology*, which noted parapsychological investigator and author Colin Wilson called "one of the scientific classics of parapsychology."

TUNING IN TO THE PAST

This exercise lets you engage your remote viewing skills to tune in to cultures from the past. Visit a museum and stand as close as you can to an artifact that sparks your curiosity. It might be a vase from the Ming Dynasty, a Bronze Age tool, or an ancient Egyptian papyrus scroll. Relax and let your conscious mind take a break, while your intuition makes a connection with this object from the past.

What do you pick up? Do you feel yourself spiraling back in history? Does your intuition present you with fragments of a prior civilization? Perhaps you'll get glimpses of life in another time. Whatever you experience—visions, emotions, sensations—can provide clues to what transpired in those bygone days.

Make notes of any impressions that come to you—landscape, weather conditions, people, housing, food, clothing, and so on. Even seemingly small or insignificant details might be meaningful. You may be able to research what you've seen and verify some of the information you've picked up, even though this knowledge lies beyond the limits of your conscious mind.

EXPLORE HISTORIC SITES PSYCHICALLY

Here's another exercise you can use to practice your ability to remotely view the past. Go to an historic building or location, perhaps an antique house, church, or battlefield. Old cemeteries are possibilities, too. Places that have not been cleaned up for public viewing are better choices than museum-like sites. If you do choose to go to a place that is frequented by tourists, avoid guided tours and visitor information booklets; you want to remain as innocent as possible about the history of this spot.

As you walk through this place that resonates with the energy of the past, allow yourself to tune in to the vibrations that permeate it. Invite all your everyday senses—sight, hearing, touch, smell, and taste—to also get involved. What do you experience?

What is the overall ambiance of this place? Do you feel comfortable or anxious here? Can you sense anything about the previous occupants? Touch your surroundings—walls, doors, windows, furnishings, artifacts, headstones, and so on. Can you pick up any information from them?

Note your impressions. If possible, attempt to verify what you've seen with your psychic vision. Visit other historic sites and repeat this exercise in psychic sensing. As you become accustomed to tuning in to your surroundings in this manner, your remote viewing skills will most likely improve.

PLAY PSYCHIC DRESS-UP

Earlier I asked if you'd ever accidentally put on someone else's coat or hat, and even though it looked like yours you somehow sensed that it was different. That's because it was imbued with the energy of another person. In this exercise, you intentionally try to pick up the vibes of a previous owner from the clothing that once belonged to him or her. Admittedly, this is harder than some of the other exercises we've done, because washing garments removes some of the energies left on them by former owners. Still, you may be able to use your remote viewing skills to intuit things that you couldn't have known consciously.

Go to a shop that specializes in vintage clothing and other period articles. Try on items that you feel attracted to, or simply hold them if they aren't your size. Purses, shoes, toiletry articles, cigarette cases, eyeglasses, and other personal objects may provide even more information than clothing because they probably haven't been laundered extensively.

Allow your intuition to time travel and pick up impressions remotely. Don't try to analyze what you experience; just go with the flow. Receive vibrations and observe flashes of insight. Try to see or sense the time and place in which these garments were initially worn, without using your rational mind. Attempt to put yourself in the former owner's place. What do you feel? Can you perceive anything about the previous owner? His or her environment? The emotions surrounding the event or situation where the clothing was worn?

If possible, try to verify your visions, feelings, and impressions. Even seemingly minor details and insights could be clues to what life was like in another time or place. You might be surprised at what you learn.

Revisit Your Past Lifetimes

The concept of reincarnation and multiple lifetimes exists in many spiritual traditions, in one form or another. We like to believe that the human race will continue on into the future, and that perhaps we will be reborn and have an opportunity to participate in those upcoming times. If reincarnation is part of your belief system, you may be curious to learn more about your past lifetimes. You can use your psychic skills to remotely view the lives you experienced before this one.

ILLUMINATE THE PAST

This exercise trains your eyes to see in a different way than usual. Before you begin remote viewing the past using this technique, I suggest that you practice gazing at a candle's flame until the technique feels comfortable for you. You can also use this method as a type of meditation.

Light a candle and place it at eye level, or as close to eye level as possible. Turn off all other forms of lighting. Begin breathing slowly and deeply, allowing yourself to relax. Focus on the flickering candle flame for as long as you can do so comfortably, then close your eyes. You should see the afterimage of the flame in your mind's eye. Keep your attention on your breathing.

When the afterimage disappears, open your eyes and look steadily at the candle again, without straining, for about thirty seconds. Then close your eyes again and see the afterimage of the flame in your mind's eye. Maintain a steady rhythm with your breathing during this time. When the afterimage fades, open your eyes and repeat the process once more. Do this exercise for about ten to fifteen minutes at a time. Practice for several days, and you'll gradually find that you are able to gaze at the candle for increasingly longer periods of time.

When you feel comfortable and confident using this technique, take it to the next level. Now it's time to remotely view your past lives, using a variation of the candle-gazing method you've been practicing. This technique comes to us from a centuries-old metaphysical organization known as the Rosicrucians.

You'll need two candles that are the same length and candleholders that will allow you to burn them safely, and a single candle to use as a focus beforehand. You'll also need a mirror. Put one candle in a candleholder on each side of the mirror. Turn off all the lights and gaze at the single candle first, as you've been doing in your practice sessions, for about five to ten minutes before you attempt to view a previous lifetime. This will enable you to quiet your mind.

When you feel ready, extinguish the single candle you were using and light the pair of candles beside the mirror. You should now be in a relaxed, peaceful state. Stare into the mirror, looking at your third eye. The third eye lies right above the bridge of the nose, on your forehead between your eyebrows. Using the mirror, continue looking intently at your third eye. Within a short time, your facial features as you view them will start to change.

Once when I used this approach I watched as my hairline receded and I actually saw a big drooping mustache on my face. My hair was pulled back into a ponytail. I felt like a Russian Cossack. Does that say something about my past, or something about a person who played a role in my family's background several generations ago?

What do you see when you do this exercise? If nothing happens for you at first, don't worry or give up. Try again in a few days.

Some of my male students have told me they saw themselves as women, and vice versa for female students. One of my students practiced this technique so often that he saw himself dressed in a full military uniform from the Civil War. He might find out some fascinating things about his predecessors if he chooses to study his family genealogy.

All of this may seem spooky to some people. It shouldn't. There are many things about life and ourselves that we have yet to discover. I promote no particular approach, philosophy, religion, or personal viewpoint. I'm simply sharing with you some avenues to explore and techniques you can use if you so desire. You'll uncover the messages and meanings for yourself as you continue to develop your psychic ability.

TAKE A STEP BACK IN TIME

Before you begin this exercise, take a few minutes to determine what you'd like to learn from going back in time to a former incarnation. Maybe you seek guidance that will help you in this lifetime.

Perhaps you'd like to understand a present-day relationship better by viewing how you and someone you know now interacted in another time and place. Or you might be dealing with a problem that you feel has roots in an earlier lifetime and want to uncover the details. Whatever your purpose, tell yourself in advance that:

- You will be safe, comfortable, and calm during your past-life regression session.
- You will remember what you experience.
- Whatever you discover will be for your benefit.

Consider having a recorder handy to capture what you describe as you witness a previous lifetime. At least keep a notebook nearby so you can write down what you experience as soon as you come out of the session.

1. Sit or lie in a comfortable place, where you will not be disturbed for at least a half hour or so. Begin by using the exercise titled "You Are More Than Your Body" in Chapter 6 to expand your consciousness beyond the limits of your present physical body. Keep stretching your awareness further and further outside your body for a few minutes.

2. When you feel ready, allow your awareness to rise up through the ceiling until you are floating above the building where you now live. Spend a moment or two looking around and enjoy seeing familiar things from this new vantage point.

3. Let yourself continue rising higher and higher, up into the sky, until you can no longer see the earth. Feel very comfortable and peaceful as you enjoy soaring above it all.

4. When you are ready, tell yourself that you will slowly descend again to earth, and when you gently land you will be in another lifetime, another body. Gradually come down from the clouds and feel yourself touch down on the earth.

5. Take a few moments to get your bearings. Then look down at your feet. What type of footwear do you have on? Often your shoes will reveal things about the period and/or locale in which you now find yourself.

6. Sense that you are in another body. What do you feel? What do you look like? You might be surprised to find that you are the opposite sex in this lifetime.

7. Gaze around you and observe the terrain, buildings, people, and so on. What do you see? Take time to notice details and things that intrigue you.

8. Just relax and let yourself move through the lifetime you are now experiencing, at a pace that's comfortable for you. See yourself doing whatever you would have done in that time and place. See the home where you lived, the family of which you were a part, the food you ate, the work you did, and so on. Don't try to control the experience, just let it evolve and go with it.

9. Ask yourself questions, such as, "What is my name?" or "Where do I live?" or "What year is it?" or "What is the purpose of this lifetime?" Perhaps you'll encounter people in this past lifetime that you know in your present incarnation, except of course they will look different and your relationship to them may be different here.

10. Gradually advance the action through time, as if you were watching a movie, allowing yourself to experience as much of this earlier life as you choose to witness. Explore

whatever you wish to explore. Learn as much as you want to learn about the period, place, and the person you were then. Spend as long as you like and go into as much depth as you like.

11. When you are ready to return to your present-day lifetime, allow yourself to again float up into the sky until you can no longer see the earth.

12. Tell yourself that you will gradually descend again into your current body, and that all is well.

13. Slowly open your eyes and give yourself time to regroup. You might feel a little disoriented at first.

14. As soon as it is comfortable for you to do so, write down or record your experiences in as much detail as possible. If you like, do some research into what you witnessed to check out the information you received and learn more about your previous lifetime.

Would you like to see in advance what's in store for you in the coming years? You can use this same technique to project yourself into the future. After expanding your awareness beyond the here and now and following the initial steps outlined above, simply tell yourself that you will descend back to earth at some date you specify in the future. You might want to start with a time in the relatively near future, say six months to a year ahead, so you'll be able to check out what you remotely view during your psychic sojourn. Then, when you've developed your time-traveling confidence, you can project further and further into the future.

Expanding the Benefits of Remote Viewing

I see potential for people to contribute to making our beloved nation more secure through remote viewing. Picture this: Certain citizens develop their psychic awareness and tap all the possible potential of their intuitive brains. By using remote viewing, they receive insights beyond what our physical vision and surveillance networks can provide, including information about what people and nations in other countries might be conjuring up against us. How awesome it would be for a band of remote-viewing experts to be able to see, sense, and predict any evil schemes and plots—as well as the mechanics of carrying them out—that enemies might be formulating against us.

On a more daily basis, think of enhanced psychic awareness as playing a role in our law enforcement and military. Could soldiers trained in remote viewing be able to determine where enemy troops might be amassed for an ambush? Or detect the location of bombs or other threats? Envision law enforcement being better equipped through psychic resources to locate missing persons, and to be able bring to justice perpetrators of crimes that baffle all other investigative resources.

Health professionals and healers, again through enhanced psychic resources, could have the ability to locate sources of illnesses—including psychological and emotional causes—and determine appropriate treatments to address them. The possibilities are endless, and certainly within our grasp. You are on the road to making this dream a reality right now.

CHAPTER RECAP

From the early 1970s until the late 1980s, the U.S. government studied the effectiveness of certain individuals to use their second sight to observe faraway places, foreign people, and situations they couldn't possibly have seen with their physical eyes. This program, conducted at the Stanford Research Institute in Menlo Park, California, discovered that it was indeed possible to use this particular type of psychic skill, termed "remote viewing," with great accuracy.

You, too, can employ your own remote viewing capabilities to glimpse other parts of the world—or even other planets—as those early psychic pioneers did. Furthermore, you can use the same skills to mentally explore the past or future. With a little practice, you can remove all the boundaries of time and distance that have limited your knowledge and experience, and use your psychic vision to go anywhere you want to go in an instant.

CHAPTER 11

The Psychic Detective

"Nowadays even presidents, vice-presidents, and heads of big agencies are opening their minds to accept psychic phenomena, because they know it works."

—Uri Geller

We tune in to the nightly news or pick up the morning newspaper and are emotionally wrenched by reports of people who have disappeared or missing children who have been abducted, leaving their frightened and confused families behind. We recoil from accounts of discovered bodies or skeletal remains of people who vanished under eerie circumstances months or even years ago. All too often, the circumstances of these disappearances or deaths remain unsolved. Guilty parties go undetected and unpunished. Questions remain. Survivors suffer.

Most police investigations these days are conducted in a sophisticated and highly professional manner. The men and women of law enforcement care; they work hard and are better trained than ever before. Electronic networks link them with their peers in thousands of departments and agencies worldwide; information is disseminated and shared almost instantaneously across states, nations, and continents. Yet so many pathways pursued and clues followed still result in dead ends.

We—you and I—can do something. For more than thirty years, I've worked with police to help them solve murders, missing persons cases, and crimes of various types. The information I offer them can't be accessed with high-tech equipment or logical research methods. However, by providing clues that I pick up using my psychic vision and the psychometry techniques I described in earlier chapters, I'm able to assist law enforcement officials in their investigations and do my part to make the world a safer, better place. You can, too.

Becoming a Psychic Detective

In early December 1979, I was invited to lecture about ESP in a town near my home in Virginia. I had been teaching a noncredit course on ESP at the University of Virginia in Charlottesville and doing private readings for a while, and was developing a reputation as a competent psychic. Although I didn't know it at the time I gave my talk, a reporter was in the audience, tape-recording my lecture.

In those days, I always did demonstrations with the audience. I had just finished my psychic demonstrations when a woman in her twenties abruptly stood up. She asked me in a trembling voice to help her sister who had been raped. She handed me a ring, which I took. Immediately, I began getting impressions and she tape-recorded what I said.

I was able to tell the young woman enough about her sister that she took the recording to the Staunton Police Department. The police contacted me a few days later and invited me to come to the victim's home. I had no previous experience working with the police, but that first case was solved and I made the local newspapers; later, the *National Enquirer* picked up the story.

The Staunton Rapist case brought me an invitation to lecture at Peninsula/Tidewater Regional Academy of Criminal Justice in Hampton, Virginia. That led to an invitation to lecture at the FBI Academy in Quantico, Virginia. I was invited back several times. At the Academy I met detectives from all over the country; some hired me to assist them with their unsolved crimes.

For the first couple of years, I flew to the crime scenes to pick up vibes. Then I learned I could stay in my office and get all the information I needed by using psychometry. In the same way I'd held the raped woman's ring at that early lecture, I could touch something police mailed to me that had belonged to a victim and receive information psychically about the crime. For about five or six years, no one knew I was working directly with detectives all over the United States.

Since then, I've become a well-known psychic and have assisted police in solving hundreds of crimes internationally. My work, although challenging, has been very rewarding. Maybe you feel drawn to become a psychic detective, too. It's certainly possible for you to do so, and to achieve success in your own right.

So You Want to Be a Psychic Detective

Perhaps you want to become a psychic detective, as many people who e-mail me do. Maybe you feel you have psychic ability and want to help others, as I have. If so, I suggest you first work hard to sharpen your skills. Start small. For example, you might help a friend find her lost cat before you offer to aid police in finding a missing person. Before you try predicting a major world crisis, try predicting the score of an upcoming ball game or election.

Work with strangers as well as friends and relatives. In fact, you may find you have more success with strangers than with people you know because you don't have other types of interpersonal connections, emotions, and past history to distract you; you can focus your energy completely on the situation at hand. Write down or record everything you see, feel, and sense as you tap in to your psychic powers. Practice, practice, practice.

I have never solicited business, nor do I encourage others to do so. Word of mouth is the best referral service and if you are good, people will come to you. I have always charged fees for my services, as any professional in any other line of business would. Most psychics, however, do not make a full-time living doing this type of work. I've been diligent, lucky, and have consistently demonstrated accuracy. If you wish to succeed, you'll need to do the same. Remember, you are dealing with people's lives and reputations, so you must be exceptionally good at what you do.

Using Psychic Detective Skills in Everyday Life

Psychic detective work is not a calling that's right for everyone. Nevertheless, you can use your psychic abilities to help yourself and others in numerous ways. By developing and fine-tuning your psychic skills, you can contribute to healing the human dramas and tragic events that plague our society.

For example, once you've sharpened your ESP, you'll know instantly if someone you meet might be dangerous to you or become a destructive influence in your life. If you notice a person checking out cars in the supermarket parking lot, you'll know if he's planning to break in to one or steal it. You could also sense possible threats that lie ahead, such as a drunk driver veering into your lane just around the next bend in the road.

These are only a few of the ways your sixth sense can come to your aid. The more aware you become of what's going on around you, the better you'll be at defusing potentially unpleasant situations and avoiding circumstances that could prove troubling for yourself and/or others.

Psychic Ability: A Powerful Investigative Tool

Many people are curious about how I work with police to help them in their criminal investigations. Let me reiterate that I do not solve crimes—the police do. I serve as an aid or an investigative tool for law enforcement officials. By picking up images and feelings the untrained mind cannot detect, I provide clues, information, and perhaps a new angle police can follow to get a break in an unsolved crime.

You need to observe certain guidelines to achieve optimal results. Over the years, I've discovered that particular techniques and practices work best for me. Here are some suggestions I offer to police and other individuals who opt to work with me, especially if this is a new investigative avenue for them.

If you decide you want to become a psychic detective, you might find these tips enable you to use your skills to best advantage. If you don't choose to follow this line of work, you can still benefit from establishing a set of guidelines and questions, so that a friend, relative, or other assistant can help to direct your psychic vision.

1. A psychic should be called into an investigation as a last resort, when traditional methods for solving a crime have been exhausted. To make a case hold in court, law enforcement officers must present hard evidence that will withstand sharp examination, questioning, and testimony from experts who present contradictory conclusions. A judge and jury aren't likely to accept testimony from a

law enforcement official who bases his entire case on clues gleaned from a psychic detective.

2. In Amber Alerts (child abduction cases) it's a good idea to call in a psychic early. The odds of finding an abducted child alive are best within the first forty-eight hours. The odds diminish as time goes on.

3. I prefer not to know any details or personal background about the victim or the crime, other than the victim's first name and the type of crime. The less someone tells me, the more I will be able to tell her. If a law officer gives me a lot of information about a case, my logical mind might kick in and start formulating answers based on reason, not intuition. I might start making assumptions or drawing conclusions, or go off in the wrong direction—all of which will interfere with my ability to psychically pick up the clues necessary.

4. I use a technique known as psychometry, a psychic skill that involves touching an object that the victim wore at the time the crime was committed, such as a piece of jewelry or a shoe, or an article that the suspect left behind. (See Chapter 9 for more information about psychometry and how it works.) Because personal objects retain the residual emotional and energetic imprint of their owners, I can hold an object the victim wore and tune in to that person's energy in order to connect with her. The same holds true for objects that belonged to the perpetrator. They resonate with his energy and I can read this energy in order to provide information about the crime.

5. One of the first things I do is try to attune my psychic sight so I can see what the victim looked like, or so I can envision the scene of the crime. I can check out these facts with

investigating officials. This first step lets me make sure I'm tuning in to the actual case or situation at hand. If I'm right, it also gives the investigating officer or agent confidence in me as a psychic.

6. The quality of an investigator's questions will affect the quality of the answers I give. The more specific and targeted a detective's questions, the better able I am to provide useful information. That's why I ask police officers to determine their precise objectives before our meeting. Do they want me to help them find a body, or a missing person? Identify a suspect? Locate a weapon? Describe what took place at a crime scene? The more keenly I can focus my mind, the more accurate I can be with my responses. Specific, relevant questions help to guide me and keep me on track.

7. The phrasing of a question is critical, too. Because I work with images and impressions that emerge or flash from the intuitive part of my mind, it's not very productive for someone to ask direct questions that probe the rational part of the brain, such as, "Where does the suspect live?" or "Did he do it?" A better approach is one that evokes an image. For example, "Stand in front of where the suspect lives and walk toward it. What you see? Look to the right, to the left, fly above it; what do you notice?" "Focus on the suspect. Look at the person. Describe what he looks like." "Describe his shirt. What kind of shoes is the person wearing?" This type of questioning helps me to focus and doesn't limit my impressions.

8. Leading questions are also unproductive. For example, if someone asks, "Is his hair black?" or "Was he driving a blue Ford?" I may be led off track or start to see the images that

have been suggested to me. I'm more successful when I can just describe the victim or suspect, and offer any other pertinent information I pick up.

9. Questions that can be answered with a yes or no don't stimulate my vision and keep the chain of images flowing. It's better to include directions, such as, "Describe what the person (or building or car) looks like."

10. Feedback is helpful, too. When I've accurately described something or someone, I like to know I'm on the right track. The logical mind can analyze, but the psychic mind just receives information. Feedback keeps my confidence up and keeps the images flowing. "Yes, I understand," is usually sufficient as an acknowledgment.

11. When I'm in a trance state and providing data, it's best if the police detective or other questioner doesn't immediately start analyzing the information I relay. I consider this part of the session as raw fact gathering and it's an opportunity for the questioner to extract as much information from me as possible. Making assumptions or decisions too quickly could interfere with the flow of impressions I'm receiving; therefore, valuable information might not come through. It's also possible that I might begin to pick up what the questioner is thinking. Therefore, I prefer that whoever questions me just gathers the information—the material can be analyzed in detail later.

12. I use all five of my physical senses to some degree. Thus, it's best if whoever questions me asks things that make use of these senses. For example, "What special sound(s) are being emitted from the house?" or "Describe any peculiar odor you smell near the building" or "What color is the car?"

13. Usually, my psychic memory is quite short. Therefore, it's important that sessions be recorded. My answers then can be replayed repeatedly or transcribed in order to detect any information that initially might have been deemed unimportant or not pertinent. My short-term memory helps me forget the disturbing emotions I feel and the upsetting sights I see and experience when I'm viewing a crime.

14. I do not claim to be 100 percent accurate in my perceptions. Nor do I claim to be able to work on all cases with an equal degree of effectiveness. You may find your own psychic ability isn't always 100 percent, either. And, like me, you will probably be better able to use your skills in some areas than in others. Everyone is unique in this regard.

Psychically Investigating Actual Crimes

Most law enforcement officials are skeptical the first time they work with me, and rightly so. In high profile cases, they get hundreds of unsolicited calls and tips from well-meaning individuals. From past experiences, I know that different people's psychic visions, dreams, and impressions vary greatly. Often, the information authorities receive from one person conflicts with other information, making it difficult to know which reports contain merit. And of course, some people who claim to be psychic are simply charlatans.

Most of the detectives I've worked with have never collaborated with a psychic before. It can be a challenge for both of us, because police usually don't understand how a psychic's mind functions. They are accustomed to dealing with hard evidence, facts, and high-tech data, not flashes of insight and impressions. That's why

I developed the guidelines I shared with you earlier (guidelines you can modify to suit your own purposes and personality). However, once I start relating information to the police—a description of the victim or the perpetrator, or details about the case that I couldn't possibly have known except through my psychic vision—they gain confidence in my ability.

When I work with a sketch artist, I describe the features and details as they come to me. As the artist puts my descriptions on paper, police officials continue to question me. I'm able to see through the victim's eyes, but can switch to seeing through the perpetrator's eyes as well. In some instances, I obtain information by remote viewing a scene from my own perspective, in response to the questions I'm asked. Sometimes the visions I receive are murky; other times they come and go very quickly. Even if I don't get a clear image, my voice continues to provide information that I pick up with my other senses. For example, I might smell an overwhelming odor or perhaps detect only a faint trace of a lingering scent. Each situation is different.

THE DOUBLE HOMICIDE OF JAKE AND DORA COHN

On May 15, 1986, Margie Cohn was talking to her mother, Dora, on the phone when she heard the gunshot that killed her mother. Only moments later, Margie's father was shot and killed. After almost three years, the double homicide remained unsolved. No murder weapon. No fingerprints. No motive. No clues.

Margie asked the detectives investigating the case to work with me. After rigorously checking me out, they called and made a phone appointment. As I've said before, I use psychometry to tune in to the people involved in a crime, so I asked them to send me something the victims had worn at the time they were shot. A few days later, a package arrived in the mail. It contained Dora's bloodied eyeglasses and her left shoe, along with Jake's belt and bloodstained shirt.

In my initial session with the police, Lieutenant Krolak of the Albany (New York) Police Department questioned me over the phone for about an hour and a half. During that time, I experienced the crime scene from both Dora's and Jake's perspectives and felt what they'd felt at the time. I immediately got an impression of the couple as being older, gray-haired, short, and I knew Jake had a prominent nose, which turned out to be correct. I sensed Dora was seated in the kitchen, talking to a female relative on the phone, and Jake was sitting in the living room watching TV when the killer entered the house. Jake, I realized, was shot in the face at close range with a handgun. Dora called out to him twice as she was struck on her upper back, and then shot in the head. I keenly felt her pain. I also saw the killer: a tall man whom the victims recognized.

The police determined I could be of assistance to them, and Lieutenant Krolak and Detective Alan Roehr flew to Orlando, Florida, where I lived at the time, to meet with me. We worked together every morning and every afternoon for four days. During one session, they asked me for the name of the killer, but I could only see his initials: R.S.

At our last session, Lieutenant Krolak pulled out ten photographs of ten suspects. I told him I didn't want to see their faces as that could affect my decision. I asked him to place the photos face down in front of me on a table. I closed my eyes and made a few passes over the photos with my hands. With little hesitation, I discarded all but three photos.

"These three are involved," I told the detectives. I picked up one, showed it to them, and said confidently, "This is the shooter."

His name was Robert Skinner. Next I turned over a photo of James Mariani, the deceased couple's grandson and Margie Cohn's son. The third photo showed Keith Snare, with whom the other two had plotted the double murder.

Based on the information gathered from hours of our taped sessions and the photo IDs, the detectives dove into the double-murder investigation with renewed enthusiasm, reviewing some old leads with a new eye. The men whose photos I selected had initially presented alibis, which police had checked out early in the investigation. They subsequently dismissed the men as suspects. However, with this new evidence, they re-examined those alibis and discovered holes in them.

It took another year for detectives to build a case against the men and arrest them. In October 1990, all three were found guilty of murder. Money turned out to be the motive. James Mariani, who masterminded the crime, erroneously believed he was a beneficiary in his grandparents' will, and had arranged to have them shot for a bundle of money he never received.

Even though the information I conveyed to the police was inadmissible in court, it provided new clues and helped them in pursuing the case. After the trial, in an interview with the *Times Union* newspaper in Albany, Lieutenant Krolak stated that working with me, a psychic, "was a different experience . . . it gave me chills." He added, "She went through the crimes . . . and described exactly what happened."

THE MURDER OF TWO CANADIAN TEENS

In 1989, Constable Moran of the Ontario Provincial Police in Thunder Bay, Ontario, Canada, watched the TV show *Incredible Sunday* about the Cohn murders and my involvement in the case. It was virtually unheard of for Canadian police to work with psychics at the time, yet Constable Moran contacted me for assistance in a double-homicide case.

As usual, I asked for articles the victims had worn at the time they were killed. Moran mailed me an earring that had belonged to one young victim and a necklace taken from another young girl's body. I gave him information about the victims, as well as descriptions of the suspect, the crime scene, the suspect's house, and his blue truck with its Goodyear tires.

My favorite sketch artist, an officer from a nearby police department, and I came up with a picture of the suspect. He and I had worked together for several years, and he always drew the face I described, usually with incredible accuracy. But Constable Moran said the sketch didn't look like any of the individuals the police considered suspects. He sent me photos of twelve men. All had dark hair and looked a little like the picture my artist friend had drawn. Nothing clicked, though. I didn't see the killer's face in the lineup.

During one of my sessions with Moran, I told him the killer would be thirty-two when he was caught, would have a mustache, and the initial R in his name. I didn't know then that he was only nineteen at the time of the murders. Thirteen years passed before technology advanced and DNA information became available. In 2000, police arrested Larry Runholm for the murder of the two teenaged girls. When Runholm was finally convicted, he was thirty-two and looked exactly like my artist friend's sketch! My clues turned out to be valid.

One of the techniques I use to locate missing persons, bodies, or other objects police are seeking—and one I availed myself of in the following case—is what I call "the clock." First I place myself at the center of an imaginary clock face. I look toward different directions, and report what I see or sense at the three o'clock position, the six o'clock position, the nine o'clock position, and so on. This enables investigators to get a 360-degree view of the site, which helps them home in on the object of their search. It's a locating device you may want to try when you're psychically looking for something that's gone missing. It doesn't have to be a person, it could be your car keys or eyeglasses. If you sense something at the one o'clock position—an airport, shopping mall, or park, for instance—that you know is actually at the three o'clock position, simply shift the clock so that site lines up and you'll notice that everything else will fall into place.

A MIAMI UNIVERSITY PROFESSOR DISAPPEARS

For me, finding a missing person is a totally different experience than working on a homicide case. When I assist police with a murder investigation, the detectives mail me something that the victim wore at the time of the crime—a ring, watch. As I described in the two real-life cases discussed above, this helps me connect with the people involved and the situation.

But when a person goes missing, everything she wore at the time goes missing with her. To try to tune in to a missing person's energy, I ask detectives to send me something she wore or used immediately prior to her disappearance. I prefer hair from a hairbrush, or the hairbrush itself, or perhaps a toothbrush—some personal item no one else would have worn or used that might have her DNA on it.

Sitting in my house hundreds or even thousands of miles away from the crime scene, talking to detectives on the phone, my job is to pinpoint where they should search for the missing person. It is critical that I not only see images of this location, but that I also communicate this information as clearly as possible to the officers. Because I tend to see disconnected images and impressions, this isn't always an easy task. And it's not an easy task for the detectives who have to connect my fragmented images.

That's all the police and I had to work with, however, when I was called in to help locate Charles Capel, a former professor at Miami University who disappeared on the evening of May 21, 2004. The eighty-one-year-old man, who suffered from Alzheimer's disease, left his home in Oxford, Ohio, and vanished. His anxious family gave me his toothbrush and a pair of his shoes to work with, so I could use my psychometry skills to connect with Professor Capel.

As I tuned in to the area where he'd lived, I could sense a rocky, rather barren area, but also tall, spiky grass and marshy ground. I also noticed a prominent stone with something written on it, but I couldn't make out the words. Psychically, I retraced the steps Capel took when he left his house and saw a fence I believed he had walked along for a short distance. The numbers 2 and 3 came into my mind, as the interviewers questioned me. This suggested Capel might have gone only about ⅔ of a mile away from his home. I also sensed he'd walked for about eight minutes, which would be consistent with that distance, and had turned left a couple times during the course of his short journey.

Although my psychic vision accurately described the area where Capel lived, which police investigators acknowledged, the details I provided weren't terribly specific. Furthermore, police had searched that area previously for the missing man to no avail, although they admitted the terrain was rugged and difficult to examine.

In January 2005, six months after the elderly man disappeared, a hunter discovered bones that turned out to be Capel's remains, less than a mile from his house. A stone marker inscribed "Stone Creek" stood nearby the spot where the remains were found. Apparently, Capel had gone out for a walk alone, had fallen, and couldn't get up. He died soon afterward.

Detective Buchholz told reporters, "People scoffed at us for seeking out a psychic's help, but Noreen's input was quite incredible . . . even a bit spooky. . . . But the body was recovered where Ms. Renier told us we would find him."

Training Police to Be Psychic Investigators

One of my goals has always been to instruct law enforcement officers in the art of psychic investigation. When I lectured at the FBI Academy in Quantico, Virginia, I realized many agents could develop their own psychic skills. I sought to train a special group who would work on cold cases and Amber Alerts. Although law enforcement officers are thoroughly trained in logical, rational techniques relating to criminal investigations, such as interrogation of witnesses, laboratory examinations, DNA analysis, fingerprint identification, and forensic processes, they can be taught to use nontraditional resources as well. Regardless of how sophisticated and high-tech investigative methods become, some crimes defy solution by the usual methods.

I aspire to teach law enforcement officers to develop their intuitive skills for crime solving. The untrained mind cannot identify certain clues. But virtually anyone can learn to sensitize and develop the natural resources that already exist within them. I train detectives in psychometry, remote viewing, psychic sensing, dream interpretation—the very same things you've been learning about in this book. These abilities perfectly complement analytical, technological investigative methods and rational thinking—in police work or in any other field of endeavor. This is my vision, and you can become an advocate and practitioner to see it realized.

How do you and I fit in? Well, as I have said repeatedly, developing your own abilities and raising your own psychic awareness will have an impact not only on you but on others as well. It will send ripples through our universe. It will contribute to the awakening in our population of the untapped potential of our brains and enhance our collective quality of life.

You may decide to go into law enforcement and broaden the capacities of investigative agencies to solve crimes, bring wrongdoers to justice, and make our world a safer place. However, you don't have to follow this path to contribute to the overall betterment of our citizenry. Your increased psychic ability can provide myriad benefits, both large and small. Perhaps you'll use your skills to locate a neighbor's lost cat, or aid your family doctor in determining the right treatment for a loved one's illness. Maybe you'll tap your heightened awareness to find the home of your dreams or a job that's perfect for you. The possibilities are endless.

I care about people. I want to help them. In the coming years, we may all be required to expand our talents beyond the ordinary channels, and to inspire others to do the same. I'm counting on you to bring your awakened psychic abilities to a level that not only benefits you, but also helps others.

CHAPTER RECAP

For more than thirty years, I've worked with police and investigators across the United States to help them solve crimes. Although in the beginning most detectives are somewhat skeptical about consulting a psychic, they usually come around after working with me for a short time. Most of my police work centers around murders and missing persons cases. In these instances, I ask police to provide me with personal objects that a victim was wearing at the time of death, or that a missing person used exclusively, such as a hairbrush or toothbrush. These objects allow me to tune in to the energies of the person(s) being sought.

Whether you're assisting police in finding a missing person or merely looking for your lost keys, utilizing your psychic sight can be a real advantage. Often I work with someone who asks me questions, in order to direct and focus my visions. In these instances, it's important that the person asks the right kinds of questions— questions that inspire insights rather than yes-or-no questions that stop the flow of information I receive intuitively, or leading questions that can put inaccurate ideas into my head. If you work with someone else to guide you in your investigative work—professionally or otherwise—it could be advantageous to devise a set of questions that will help you arrive at the answers you seek.

Although your second sight probably won't be accurate 100 percent of the time, it should be at least 75 to 80 percent correct. You may be more effective in some circumstances than others, but with practice you'll improve your psychic abilities in all areas. By doing so, you'll contribute to the betterment of not only yourself and your loved ones, but all of humanity as well.

CHAPTER 12

Ghosts and Poltergeists

"There are an infinite number of universes existing side by side and through which our consciousnesses constantly pass. In these universes, all possibilities exist. You are alive in some, long dead in others, and never existed in still others. Many of our 'ghosts' could indeed be visions of people going about their business in a parallel universe or another time—or both."

—Paul F. Eno, *Faces at the Window*

Even with all the advances in this electronics age, we still have no scientific methods to either definitively prove or disprove the existence of ghosts. But that doesn't quash for one moment the debate and speculation, nor calm the ardor of those who believe in ghosts and those who vehemently reject the idea.

For centuries, stories of ghosts, apparitions, and the appearance of visitations from the dead have existed in cultures around the world. Many of our greatest writers, including Shakespeare (in *Hamlet*) and Dickens (in *A Christmas Carol*), have vividly shared their characterizations of ghosts. The website *www.angels ghosts.com* posts hundreds of stories and intriguing photos taken by people who believe they've personally witnessed the presence of ghosts. Various organizations and groups—you may have one or even several in your state—claim to be able to visit the site of a reported haunting and, with the aid of various electronic devices, prove or disprove the presence of a ghost or an apparition.

Do ghosts exist? In my career as a professional psychic, I have investigated numerous hauntings for private individuals, businesses, and scientific institutes. I have experienced enough to acknowledge the real possibility of the presence of what I'll call "otherworldly inhabitants." I've included two of my case histories below. My interactions with these otherworldly inhabitants have led me to some personal conclusions:

- I absolutely believe that people experience encounters with nonphysical apparitions.
- I also believe those apparitions, or ghosts, are actually a form of energy.

Energy can't be destroyed. When we die, our energy continues on even though our physical bodies have deteriorated. I think this is the energy that causes what we call "hauntings." Does that mean when we die we all become ghosts? Not necessarily. However, I conclude that several factors can create the entities we label "ghosts."

Why Ghosts Haunt the Living

Like living people, ghosts have purposes for their behavior. They don't just appear capriciously, nor do they get a kick out of scaring people. Psychic Karl Petry, who has seen ghosts of the dead since he was a child, explained to me that in his experience with ghosts, "the strongest thing that often comes through is a very deep sense of loneliness. Many ghosts were lonely in life. They are still lonely in death."

Ghostly hauntings usually occur for one of three reasons. At times, these categories may overlap.

1. The most common type of haunting is caused by a ghost who doesn't realize he or she is dead. For these individuals, death came swiftly and unexpectedly. Perhaps he was a farmer suddenly struck by lightning on his way home from working in the fields. Unaware of his death, he returns home in the form of energy. His presence is felt by his family members, his footsteps heard, his pipe smoke smelled. This type of haunting usually fades away as the entity comes to realize he is physically dead.

   Ghosts and apparitions are often said to appear at battlefields. At these places of violence, soldiers were alive one moment and cut down an instant later, without being able to properly prepare for death. People who die in car crashes and other types of unexpected accidents also may fall into this category of ghosts.

2. Sometimes ghosts result when a person is pulled back by earthly ties such as an obsessive habit, an inordinate desire, or an attachment to something or someone. For example, someone who has spent his life fixing up and enjoying his house may literally refuse to leave it.

   In 1943, while he was still a young man in basic training during World War II, Dr. George G. Ritchie, MD, died of double lobar pneumonia. Nine minutes later, unaccountably, he returned to life. While clinically dead for those nine minutes, Dr. Ritchie journeyed in spirit to numerous places he had been to while alive.

In his book *Return from Tomorrow*, he writes about an amazing experience of watching the ghosts of deceased alcoholics in a bar, unseen by the living patrons around them. "Then I noticed a striking thing. A number of the men standing at the bar seemed unable to lift their drinks to their lips. Over and over I watched them clutch at their shot glasses, hands passing through the solid tumblers, through the heavy wooden countertop, through the very arms and bodies of the drinkers around them." The ghosts' addiction to alcohol bound them to the earth plane and specifically to places where alcohol was served.

3. In some instances, a ghost needs to communicate something she forgot to say or needed to say while embodied, perhaps to a loved one, an enemy, or someone else. Suicides and murder victims are most common in this type of haunting. The disembodied entity is trying to get the attention of someone, perhaps to convey important information the living person needs to know. When my friend Candy was fourteen, she and her sister both saw the ghost of their father's first wife, whom they'd never known in life. The woman had come to tell them that their father would soon die and they would lose their home. A murder victim who was denied justice may want to communicate his feelings regarding this injustice or provide information about his murderer, and cannot rest until the dire deed is rectified or avenged.

Ghosts can take on various forms and communicate in many different ways. Once a new client wanted to know about her daughter's death. I was about to explain that I only work with law enforcement officers on homicide cases, but suddenly, I *was* her daughter, telling the bereaved mother what had happened. Perhaps the mother's desperate need to know what had transpired enabled the daughter's ghost to speak through me.

Communicating with Ghosts

Not all ghosts are perceived as annoying, nor do they cause dismaying disturbances in the lives of the people they knew while they lived on earth. Some ghosts are rather benign, even friendly. In some instances, the people left behind welcome the ghostly presence of former friends and loved ones.

Nor do all ghosts appear in the same way to living people. Not every ghost will pound on your walls and ceilings, or jump out of a closet and shout, "Boo." Most of us think of ghosts as physical manifestations, but that's not true. Some of them come to you in dreams, realizing you probably won't notice them during the day when you're preoccupied with mundane things. Others materialize in your mind as thoughts. They may even present themselves to you as aromas. A woman I know senses the presence of her sister's ghost when she smells the perfume her sister wore, even though no one seems to be there.

Talking to Ghosts

If you wish, you can talk to the ghosts of relatives and friends. My mother was very close to her brother, who died of cancer, and she missed him desperately. Therefore, she took time regularly to talk with him. She set aside a special time and a specific place where she sat and communicated with him mentally. She listened to the responses that came into her head, never doubting that these were her brother's thoughts and his answers to her questions. However, during a period when she was very busy moving, she let those regular talks slide. About that time, one of my daughters was visiting her and practicing psychometry with my mother's ring. "Your brother wants you to contact him again," she told my mother. "He misses your talks."

My daughter didn't remember that my mother's brother had died the previous year, and she certainly wasn't aware that her grandmother regularly spoke to the deceased brother. My mother burst into tears, never realizing how much those talks meant to her brother on the other side.

Steps for Contacting a Deceased Person

You've probably heard of séances, during which people who have lost loved ones attempt to contact those individuals with the assistance of a medium. Séances became popular in the United States and England during the Victorian period, and at different times throughout history they have gained and lost favor. Of course, many of the mediums who conducted these sessions turned out to be frauds. That doesn't discount the validity of communication with deceased beings, however.

If you want to contact a deceased friend or family member, you don't need a go-between. I suggest taking the following steps:

1. Set up a specific time to communicate with your departed loved one. If you don't make contact immediately, don't become discouraged. It might take two or three sessions before he responds. Remember, this is new territory for both of you.

2. Write down questions you want to ask this person. Organize and prioritize them. Be specific.

3. Enter into the session with respect, faith, and sincerity. Trust that you will connect with the person with whom you wish to communicate. Believe the thoughts and impressions that come into your head during this session are your loved one's way of speaking to you—not just your imagination. How else can your departed friends and relatives communicate?

4. Hold a photograph of the person you wish to contact, or an item he wore or used (such as clothing, jewelry, eyeglasses, or a pipe).

5. Light a candle or two. Relax, perhaps by doing some deep breathing practices. Meditate, using a designated meditation that you'll only use when you want to make contact with that person.

6. You might find it easier to write down what you feel the deceased is communicating to you by using the technique known as automatic writing. To do this, temporarily set your rational, logical mind aside and open your intuitive mind to the person you wish to contact. Close your eyes, and on a piece of paper write whatever you feel inspired to write. Don't worry about whether it makes sense or even if you can read what you've written; just let yourself be guided.

7. Knocks on the wall or a table are another way to communicate. This is easiest if you ask only yes-or-no questions. Explain to the spirit the code you've determined, such as one knock means no, and two knocks means yes. Ask a yes-or-no question, and then listen for knocks that convey your loved one's answers.

My psychic friend Karl Petry has found that music can help to attract a nonphysical entity. He recommends softly playing a song from the time period when the person died, over and over, while you call out the person's name. I suggest experimenting with these techniques to see which ones prove most effective for you. Note that you may need to use different practices to connect with different entities; like living people, ghosts have unique personalities, dispositions, preferences, and styles of communication.

A SUICIDE'S GHOST HAUNTS A FRIEND

Early in my career as a psychic, my friend Ron asked me to try to contact a close friend of his named Jimmy who had recently committed suicide. Eager to help a friend, I arrived at Ron's house one evening to try to establish a connection between Ron and Jimmy.

I settled into a comfortable chair; Ron sat nearby on his sofa. I quickly entered into a deep trancelike state, and contacted Jimmy. In the beginning, I served as the go-between, allowing Ron to talk to Jimmy through me and relaying Jimmy's answers to Ron's questions. Soon, Jimmy began using my voice to speak directly to Ron. It was clear that the love between these two friends had been strong and that much had been left unsaid.

I felt drained when I awoke from the trance. Exhausted, I went home immediately. A few hours later, Ron called, desperate. He said strange things were happening in his house—loud thumps on the wall and ceiling, which kept him awake. When the refrigerator began shaking, he decided it was time to leave the house.

He came to my place and nervously paced back and forth in my living room. He asked me, "Would you please spend the night at my house alone tomorrow and stop Jimmy from creating these disturbances?" Not really knowing what I could do or how to do it—I was still inexperienced in this line of work—I nonetheless felt I had to give it a try.

The next night it felt eerie being alone in Ron's house, but after the tiring events of the previous night I was eager to get to bed and grab some welcomed sleep. I hoped Jimmy was gone, but no such luck. Noises on the walls and ceilings broke out as soon as my head hit the pillow. Obviously I was not alone. At first I tried to ignore this presence. But as the noise grew consistently louder and more insistent, an image of Jimmy's face loomed into my mind.

Exhausted and exasperated, I cried out, "Jimmy, please, I'm so tired. I need to sleep. Would you be a dear and come back tomorrow night?" I felt the presence depart. Almost immediately I fell into a long, peaceful sleep. I awoke in the morning, refreshed. I dressed hastily, thanked the ghost, just in case he was still around, and left the house.

When Ron returned, Jimmy was still there, and he resumed pounding on doors and shaking Ron's appliances. Again, the walls and ceilings trembled. Clearly, the presence was trying to get attention.

The following evening, I went back to Ron's house. This time I was rested and had more energy. But Jimmy also had more energy because my contact with him the previous night had strengthened and intensified his earth-bound ties.

I gently explained to Jimmy, communicating mind to mind, that he had created his own death. It had been his decision, his choice. I told him he must accept it. I further explained that he no longer belonged on this plane of existence; he must release his earthbound ties and accept the next phase that awaited him. I told him the people here loved him and would always love him. But he had new experiences waiting for him and must accept the next phase.

Mentally, I searched around Jimmy for loved ones on the nonphysical plane, people he had known previously and who had died years prior to his suicide. I assured him they would lead him to the other world. Jimmy, with help from these guides, apparently found the light and peace that awaited him. He never returned.

Ghostly Hangouts

Where are ghosts most active? Do they tend to gather at certain spots, such as cemeteries, or at certain times of the month or year, such as Halloween? Do such things as "Club Dead" ghost resorts or ghost conventions exist? Although we don't have definitive scientific proof, some patterns do emerge when it comes to ghostly sightings.

Humid Places

According to the Association for the Scientific Study of Anomalous Phenomena in the United Kingdom, which has been investigating paranormal phenomena since 1981, people report the presence of ghosts more often in damp, low-pressure areas than in sunny, dry ones. The entities perceived may be the spirits of deceased mortals, as some people believe, or a type of energy pattern. High humidity may account for the prevalence of ghost sightings in England and Ireland, countries notorious for their rainy, low atmospheric pressure climates. Ghosts are not reported as appearing with equal frequency in areas with dry, high-pressure sunny climates, such as the Mediterranean countries and Mexico.

In the United States, more ghost reports come from hot, humid states, such as South Carolina and Louisiana, as well as from cold, wet states, such as Maine and Massachusetts, than hot, dry states such as Arizona, Utah, or Nevada. The clichéd "dark and stormy night" atmosphere of many supernatural books and movies may not be so far off after all.

Battlefields and Disaster Areas

Places where large numbers of people died—often suddenly and/or unexpectedly—seem to be common spots for ghosts to gather. Gettysburg, Pennsylvania, for example, is home to numerous notoriously haunted locales including The Angle, where 10,000 Confederate soldiers died in an hour-long battle and where Robert E. Lee's ghost has been spotted. The Tower of London, the site of many executions, murders, and tortures, also has its share of ghosts—even Anne Boleyn is said to show up on the anniversary of her execution, carrying her severed head under her arm.

The Shadowlands, a website of haunted places around the world (*http://theshadowlands.net*), lists San Antonio, Texas, as one of the most haunted places in the United States. The Alamo, where 189 Alamo defenders and approximately 1,200 Mexican soldiers died, is San Antonio's most famous haunted site. The Emily Morgan Hotel, where soldiers wounded at the Alamo were treated, appears to be haunted as well. The city also features many other colorful ghosts including Teddy Roosevelt and a number of his Rough Riders at the Menger Hotel, and the disgruntled "Beatrice" who turns on kitchen faucets and throws around utensils at the Cadillac Bar.

THE CASE OF THE HAUNTED SPA

Although the usual setting for a ghost story is a rambling and dilapidated Victorian house, a drafty castle, or a musty, magnolia-draped antebellum mansion, in actuality people generally report ghosts in more mundane places. Billerica, Massachusetts, for instance, claims to have a haunted Burger King.

One day while I was engaged in experiments for the Psychical Research Foundation in Durham, North Carolina, a parapsychologist named Joan pulled me aside. "Will you have time this evening to investigate a haunted business?" she asked me.

At this early stage of my career, I was always willing to try anything that might improve my developing psychic awareness. "I'll go," I replied. "What type of business would be haunted?"

"Sorry," she said, "but I can't tell you anything. In fact, just to make sure you don't use telepathy, the boss is only sending those of us who don't know anything about the haunting."

Late that night, Joan, her two assistants, and I piled into a small car, crammed inside with several recording and monitoring devices. Fortunately, the business was only a few miles away. When we turned into a modern shopping center, I thought, *Oh, no! Not a haunted Food Lion*, but we drove past the supermarket and parked in front of a health spa. *A haunted spa?* I wondered.

We unloaded the car and entered a reception room where two worried-looking young women in leotards awaited us. They gave us a quick tour of the facility, and then settled us in the middle of an exercise room. We hoped to contact the spirit and learn why it was haunting the spa. The two young employees were clearly excited, but also anxious about what might happen.

We had plenty of recording equipment set up, but I felt I needed some paper and a pen. I rarely used automatic writing (a technique that involves becoming a channel for a spirit who communicates a message that the channeler, while in a trance, writes down), but I was learning to trust my instincts. One of the employees brought me a notepad and pen, and we began.

The six of us sat in a circle on the highly polished hardwood floor. I relaxed and led the group in some deep-breathing exercises. Soon I entered an altered state of consciousness. I found myself watching a woman who seemed to be in her late fifties. She was sitting in swirling, bubbling water, her flaming red hair floating wildly on the surface. Suddenly, she grabbed her chest and cried out.

I opened my eyes and said, "An older woman with dyed red hair died in your whirlpool bath."

The two spa employees looked at each other blankly. They had only worked there for a short time and couldn't verify anything I had witnessed.

Joan took charge. "Noreen, go back in and tell us more."

I closed my eyes again and immediately more images poured into my mind. "She's upset," I said. "She's very demanding. I keep seeing water overflowing. She's telling me she's been trying to communicate with people at the spa. She keeps phoning, but they don't hear her when they answer the phone. Sometimes you hear her on the back steps leading to the women's locker room."

Impulsively, I picked up the pad and pen and began writing. My eyes were still closed so I had no idea what I was writing. The information bypassed my conscious mind and went straight through my hand to the paper. Almost as suddenly as it started, the writing stopped. Once again I was listening to this angry woman and repeating her words: "You tell my attorney to get going. He's had too many delays, too many interruptions. Tell him to finish my case." I could feel her agitated emotions in my own body as she added, "I'd like to tell him a thing or two."

Suddenly, I was jarred back to reality as all four phone lines started ringing simultaneously in the offices—but no one was on the phone. I was getting tired, so we decided to stop. Joan took the notepad on which I'd written three names.

Later, I learned the whole story from Dr. William Roll, director of the Psychical Research Foundation (sponsored by Duke University) and an expert in poltergeist phenomena who has authored four books on the subject. The names I'd written on the pad were those of the dead woman, her husband, and her lawyer. The woman had been a member of the health spa, and apparently, she had been just as acerbic in life as she was in death. She had indeed suffered a fatal heart attack in the whirlpool bath.

Soon after, the haunting started. Every Wednesday, the whirlpool would overflow at a specific time—the day and hour she had died. The water stopped as mysteriously as it started, and plumbers couldn't find a problem to fix. At the same time, the phone would ring, but no one was ever on the line. The telephone company checked the phones, but found nothing wrong. Almost all of the spa instructors had heard footsteps on the back stairs, which usually began just before the spa closed. Members who were there late also heard the sounds.

The husband had filed suit against the spa, but the attorney who was handling the case and the woman's will had delayed settling it to attend to other pressing matters. Now, with this new information, the husband urged the lawyer to finish. When the case was finally settled, the haunting stopped.

How to Get Rid of an Unwanted Ghost

Are you troubled by eerie footsteps on the stairs when no one is there? Do you often feel an inexplicable tingling on the back of your neck? Would you rather keep the lights on in your house at night because you fear the dark? Have you felt the presence of something you can't define, or heard pings or taps on the wall that seem to have no obvious source? If so, it's conceivable you have stirred up something in your house, whether you live in an old building or a new one. If this worries you, you can take steps to get rid of an unwanted ghost.

In my professional career, I have frequently been asked to try to rid locations of ghosts or apparitions. Each incident has to be handled differently according to the type of haunting and the participants involved. Sometimes I have had success at sending the haunting presence on its way. Sometimes I've failed. Much depends on the temperament of the person or persons being haunted, the personality of the ghost and its purpose, and the physical environment.

If ghostly intruders trouble you, if you're pestered or downright frightened by an otherworldly specter, let me suggest some possible approaches you can take.

1. Ignore the ghost, if you can. Pay no attention to the bangs, pings, rattling, and other manifestations of a ghostly intruder. I realize that accepting this may be easier said than done. Ghosts seldom intend violence, however, or wish you harm.

2. If the trouble persists and you cannot ignore nor tolerate the situation, then attempt to contact the ghost. You may be able to do this directly, through your own mind, or you might seek the assistance of a medium. Try to discover what the ghost wants: What are the factors motivating her contact with you and/or other living persons?

   Be aware, however, that this approach can make the ghost's earthly ties stronger. Not all ghosts want to hang around permanently; they have a message or something important to relay, and nothing more. But some ghosts do want to remain connected to their old lives and the people they knew when they were alive. By paying attention to ghosts, living individuals give them energy that can strengthen the ghosts' earthly ties.

3. When all else fails, exorcise the ghost. If you don't feel up to this yourself, contact a parapsychologist, a psychic research center, or clergy member.

Conducting Your Own Exorcism

You've determined that a house, place of business, or other site is haunted by the presence of a ghostly being. The entity shows no indication of leaving. How do you get rid of this presence? Most ghosts, as I've said before, do not intend harm or mayhem, so in most cases you won't be in any type of danger. Here's a technique you can use to clear the air, so to speak, and send the entity on its way.

1. Light a bundled wand of sage or a stick of sage incense. If possible, walk in a clockwise direction around the perimeter of the area where the ghost abides, carrying the burning sage so that the smoke trails behind you. When you've completed the circle, return to its center. Then walk through the house, building, or other space while holding the burning sage wand or incense stick. Allow the smoke to waft through the space and cleanse it. This is called "smudging" and it clears the energy of the area.

2. Envision yourself surrounded by a ball of pure white light that protects you and keeps you safe from all potential dangers. If you like, say aloud something like, "I am surrounded by divine white light. I am safe and sound at all times and in all situations."

3. Call out to the ghost, by name if you know what name it went by in its last physical lifetime. Allow time for it to make itself known, and for you to sense its presence.

4. When the entity appears—assuming it behaves in a peaceful manner—ask it what it wants and give it a chance to relay its intention to you. You may receive this information

in one of many ways: hearing, seeing, feeling, smelling, or just *knowing* what the ghost wants to communicate to you.

5. After learning what the ghosts wants or needs, acknowledge and respect it. If the ghost is trying to convey a message, and you understand that message, say so. If the message is for someone else, agree to pass the information along to the proper person(s). You may want to note the ghost's purpose for showing up and address this later, if you can.

6. Mentally or verbally explain to the entity that it no longer exists on the earth plane. The ghost may not realize it isn't physical anymore, especially if death came suddenly and unexpectedly.

7. If you can, mentally envision a tunnel of white light leading from this place to a peaceful, nonphysical realm—what some might call heaven or the hereafter or Nirvana. Direct the ghost to this light and tell it to go to the light that awaits it. Assure the ghost that all will be well, that it's safe to follow this path. Be kind, but firm in commanding it to go away.

8. If you know people to whom the ghost was related when embodied on the earth plane, you may see the spirits of these individuals and point them out to the ghost. Tell the ghost that these beings will shepherd it to the place where it belongs now, and where it will be at peace. Bless the entity as you send it on its way.

9. When you feel confident that the ghost has departed, retrace your initial steps around the perimeter of the space, but this time move in a counterclockwise direction. Sprinkle salt or saltwater on the ground in a circle as you walk, in order to purify the ground and establish a barrier that will prevent the ghost from returning.

10. If you are in a house or other building, open all the windows
and let fresh air cleanse the space. If you've been conduct-
ing this ritual at night, turn on the lights and let them flood
the area with brightness for a while. Feel thankful, relaxed,
and peaceful, confident that the ghost has moved on to its
proper place and that you will no longer be troubled by its
presence.

Are There Animal Ghosts?

Long ago I had a small black poodle named Fifi, whom I loved
dearly. My neighbor at the time, a kindhearted woman named
Martha, had a small white poodle she called Muffin Sue. Martha
often invited Fifi over to visit her dog, and the dogs were like kids
playing together.

One day a car ran over and killed my beloved dog. About a
week later, I thought I heard a faint barking and Fifi's familiar
scratching at my bedroom door. This continued for about four or
five days. My sister, who lived with me, heard the scratching and
the barking, too, but thought it was her imagination.

Martha called me the same week Fifi died. She'd moved away
and didn't know he was dead. However, she'd had a vivid dream
about him that was so beautiful she wanted to share it. In the
dream, she saw Fifi leaping in an open field with a bright ray of
sunlight surrounding her like a spotlight.

Do animals have souls? Do they show up as ghosts after they
die, as Fifi seemed to have done? Do they reincarnate? I'm not
sure anyone knows the answers to those questions. People who
lose their beloved pets often believe they'll be reunited with their
furry companions after their own deaths. Most mainstream reli-

gions deny that animals have souls. I do believe that animals, like humans, are energy and when they die that energy does not disappear. Are the animals we loved so much in life waiting for us at a Rainbow Bridge? I simply don't know, but I can't say "absolutely not."

Poltergeists

Poltergeists are not to be confused with ghosts. The word *poltergeist* is German for "noisy ghost." In my opinion, however, this is a misnomer because no ghost is actually involved.

In poltergeist cases, objects are thrown about or moved by unseen forces, almost always when a certain individual is present. The energies of this particular person are the source of the disruptions. A living person—not the ghost of someone dead—is responsible for the movements and physical disturbances. He or she is creating the disturbances unconsciously.

The types of disturbances that occur during poltergeist activity vary. Sometimes simple rapping and pinging sounds can be heard on the walls or furniture. Other times objects slide across tables or even appear to launch themselves around the room. Objects may disappear completely, or reappear in unusual places. Lights and appliances may turn themselves on and off, or stay on even when you shut them off.

Adult Poltergeists
Usually we think of poltergeist problems in connection with adolescents; however, adults can produce this type of disturbance, too. When an adult is responsible for poltergeist disturbances, she is usually experiencing a stress-related or frustrating situation or relationship. Conscious suppression of hostility or another type

of stress may be at the root of the poltergeist activity. The reaction to the stress is a subconsciously directed outburst—the person doesn't know herself that she's causing the disturbance. You could call it a subconscious temper tantrum.

Adolescent Poltergeists

When a young person or an adolescent (even someone as old as midtwenties) is involved in causing the disturbance, the physical stress of puberty and the accompanying psychological stress are usually the cause. Sometimes the young person has learned or been forced to suppress strong emotions. The "too good" little boy or girl who hasn't been able to vent emotions often has a volcano of frustration bubbling inside, which can erupt into psychic energy.

In most poltergeist cases, there are no immediate solutions. Understanding who is causing the phenomenon, though, is the first step toward resolving the disturbance. It could be helpful for that person to learn normal ways to release tension and frustration. A counselor, psychologist, or psychiatrist who is knowledgeable about such experiences may be able to help the person handle the problem.

Other Differences between Poltergeists and Ghosts

Although ghostly hauntings often continue for long periods of time—sometimes for centuries—poltergeist activity is relatively short-lived, usually lasting less than a few months. Perhaps a change in the person's situation causes the stress or anger behind the poltergeist energy to diminish, and thus the disturbances cease.

Ghosts, as I said earlier, tend to be lonely beings, but poltergeists are often quite sociable. You aren't likely to find poltergeist phenomena occurring in a cemetery or a remote area where an historic battle took place. Instead, the activity of poltergeists usually goes on in the family home and in the presence of the person to whom the poltergeist energy is attached. After all, that individual is, in fact, causing the disturbances and he is subconsciously looking for attention.

A PERSONAL POLTERGEIST EXPERIENCE

Sometimes we use the expression "it rained cats and dogs" in describing a strong thundershower. But in Florida, where it can rain as in no other state, the term is more often "frog strangler." That's what pounded my old Ford that evening. Rain came down in sheets, rendering the windshield wipers useless. I couldn't see in front of me, out the side windows, or behind. It was like trying to drive my car while underwater, only I had no sonar, no radar.

I was too nervous to see the humor in this scenario. Here I was, a psychic, en route to conduct a séance. Like a scene from a horror movie, thunder and lightning punctuated my arrival at my clients' home. Sue and Jan, my clients, awaited me on the porch and greeted me almost timidly. They had invited me to help them contact a friend who had committed suicide, but they now seemed uncertain, even frightened.

The pair fluttered about like moths as we entered their small living room. I glanced around, dismayed by what I saw. Sue and Jan had displayed religious pictures and crucifixes not only on the walls, but propped upon tables, even on the floor leaning against the worn furniture. Crosses, cheap reproductions of Jesus, holy scenes, and inscriptions surrounded me. I got the feeling the women were trying to ward off something they perceived as evil.

We lit candles and turned off the lights. We all meditated and I relaxed into a trance state. Soon I made contact with their dead friend, Bob. Bob explained his feelings of hopelessness, and that he had needed to leave the world of the living. His inability to honestly share his feelings with his friends while alive multiplied his frustrations and anxieties, something I've found to be the case with most suicides I have encountered. His homosexuality had added to his emotional burden. Bob's fear of life had been greater than his fear of death.

I was extremely tired after the séance, and tried unsuccessfully to bring the evening to an end. But Jan and Sue were charged up and insisted we have coffee and dessert. They chattered on about psychic experiences and bombarded me with questions. I tried to reach their subconscious minds by silently crying out, "Please get me out of here, let me leave!" But to no avail. A few minutes later I repeated the thought with even more intensity. Again, nothing happened.

Suddenly, their dog sat up and looked at the front door, bristled, and growled. The doorbell rang. We all looked at each other. Who could be ringing the doorbell at this time of night? Sue flicked on the porch light and opened the door, leaving the chain hooked. No one could be seen. She removed the chain and opened the door. The women went out onto the porch with the dog, but no one was there. No sooner had they come back into the house than the doorbell rang again. Now frightened, Sue started to shut the door, but the bell rang again.

While the door was open, I seized the opportunity and left. Driving home, I realized my desperate plea had been heard after all. *I* was responsible for the doorbell ringing. We all can create poltergeist phenomena with our minds under the right circumstances.

CHAPTER RECAP

Energy can't be destroyed. When we die, our energy continues on even though our physical bodies have deteriorated. I think this energy produces what we call ghosts. Ghosts usually visit the earth plane for one of three reasons: they don't know they are dead; they have information to deliver to someone living; or they retain a strong attachment to someone or something in the physical world and are reluctant to move on.

Ghosts tend to show up with greater frequency in humid places, although science cannot explain exactly why. They also appear at sites where many people have died quickly or unexpectedly, such as disaster areas or battlefields. Many hundreds of locales around the world are notoriously haunted—not just spooky old castles and crumbling mansions, but ordinary modern places as well. If a ghost seems to be haunting you, you can take steps to send it on its way. If, however, your ghost is friendly and/or you wish to communicate with the spirit of a departed loved one, that's possible, too.

Don't confuse poltergeists with ghosts. Poltergeist phenomena arise from repressed anger or stress within a living person. The subconscious emotion often expresses itself outwardly by moving objects or making noises. Not only adolescents generate poltergeist activity; adults can as well.

CHAPTER 13

The Psychic Realm of Dreams

"We are not only less reasonable and less decent in our dreams . . . we are also more intelligent, wiser and capable of better judgment when we are asleep than when we are awake."

—Erich Fromm

Why do we dream? Where do dreams come from? And what do they mean anyway? Questions such as these have baffled humankind for millennia. The spiritual texts of many cultures abound with accounts of dreams and their significances. The Bible, for instance, recounts such colorful stories as Jacob's dream of angels climbing a ladder to heaven, and the Israelite Joseph interpreting the Egyptian Pharaoh's prophetic dream about fat and lean cattle. Literature and art draw upon dreams extensively, too. Who hasn't delighted in Shakespeare's *A Midsummer Night's Dream* or marveled at the dream-inspired surrealistic paintings of Salvador Dali? Scientists and shamans, philosophers and psychiatrists all probe and ponder the dream world, yet the debate about the origin and purpose of dreams continues.

Dreams and the Psychic Realm

Dreams appear to be linked to the psychic realm. Many dream researchers and psychoanalysts believe our dreams are the sub-conscious' way of communicating with us. Often dreams help us process the events of the day, or work through the prob-lems in our waking lives. Sometimes they provide answers to questions and concerns that the conscious, analytical mind can't resolve. Dreams offer a vehicle for the subconscious to reveal hidden dynamics in our psyches. They guide, inspire, enlighten, and entertain us—and occasionally give us glimpses of the future.

A DREAM REVEALS EVIDENCE TO A MURDER

Once, back in the days when I used to visit crime scenes, a dream helped me find the murder weapon in a homicide case. The victim had been shot. Using psychometry, I described the suspect and did my usual work on the case. But although the police asked me several times where the weapon was, I could not pick up any information.

I had to stay overnight before flying home the next day. That night I had a dream in which I saw the suspect hiding the gun in a flower box. I'd gone to the victim's home the day before and the house in my dream reminded me of the one where the murdered person had lived. I remembered having seen a flower box beside the front door.

At first I was reluctant to give the detectives information I'd obtained from a dream. I had never gotten information about a case in this manner. What if my dream was wrong? However, on the way to the airport, I finally decided to tell them what I'd dreamed. They said they would check it out and let me know if they found anything. When I got home I found a message from the detective on my answering machine—they found the gun in the flower box!

Dreams can be a powerful way to connect with the intuitive part of your brain. If you haven't been paying much attention to your dreams, or if you usually don't remember your dreams at all, now is the time to change that.

Everyone Dreams Every Night

You dream every night, usually for a total of about an hour and a half, even if you don't remember your dreams. Dreams occur during what's known as REM sleep. The term, coined in the mid-twentieth century by Nathaniel Kleitman, professor of physiology at the University of Chicago, and his student, Eugene Aserinsky, refers to the rapid eye movements that take place when you are dreaming.

If you're like most adults, you have between three and five dreams per night, with each dream lasting from a few minutes to half an hour or longer. You are influenced by your dreams, consciously or subconsciously, whether or not you remember them. Kleitman and Aserinsky found that when people were awakened every time they entered the REM stage and weren't allowed to dream, they became irritable and anxious. In his book *Dreamlife*, David Fontana suggests that "we sleep partly *in order to dream.* Sleep . . . may be the servant of the dream."

Swiss analyst Carl G. Jung considered dreams to be a means to alert the dreamer to hidden facets about himself, and they acted to correct one-sided development of personality. In *Civilization in Transition*, he wrote, "The dream is a little hidden door in the innermost and most secret recesses of the soul."

I've heard that phases of a person's nature are revealed in his dreams for the express purpose of directing him to higher, more balanced accomplishments; a lofty goal. The inspiration Einstein received in a dream, for example, led him to develop his theory of relativity, and artist Paul Gauguin's dreams gave him ideas for his paintings.

Types of Dreams

Although the content and tone of your dreams may take myriad forms, all dreams can be categorized into one of five basic types. In some instances, they may overlap and contain more than one theme.

Emotional Release Dreams

The most common type of dream for the majority of people, emotional release dreams are the subconscious' way of expressing fear, anger, joy, and other emotions. Feelings you repress consciously or experiences you find too difficult to deal with directly will most likely play themselves out in your dream dramas. If, for example, you feel angry and frustrated in your workplace, but can't show this emotion because you need the job, you might release the pent-up stress while you sleep. This type of dream can serve a cleansing, freeing purpose for your psyche.

Upon waking, pay attention to the emotions in your dream, not just the actions that take place. Because dreams speak in symbols, the literal events in the dream probably won't resemble the daytime situations they represent. A dream about feeling anxious because you're driving a car and can't see through the windshield may suggest you feel anxious because you don't know where you're headed in your life. Can you identify areas in your waking life in which you feel the same kind of emotions you encountered in the dream? This could be the key that lets you unlock the door to your inner wisdom and deal with the difficulties you're undergoing.

Problem-Solving Dreams

In a frequently told story, Elias Howe, who invented the lock-stitch sewing machine, had been trying for years to perfect his design. One night he dreamed he'd been captured by cannibals, who planned to eat him if he didn't come up with the solution. Howe noticed the cannibals held spears with holes near the pointed ends. That image provided the missing piece of the puzzle that he needed: he placed the hole near the point in the sewing machine's needle and it worked.

Many famous people, including Benjamin Franklin and Thomas Edison, were known to sleep on it when faced with a problem. Often they got answers to their daytime conundrums from their dreams. You've probably had the same experience. Maybe you've been trying to solve a dilemma using the analytical, logical part of your brain, but without success. Dreams give you access to the creative, intuitive part of the mind where the solutions lie.

You can even program yourself to problem solve while you sleep. When you go to bed, think about the problem for a few moments before you drift off and tell yourself you will have a dream that provides the information you need. It may take several nights before you get the answer, but keep trying. Once your subconscious gets used to receiving your commands it will quickly respond with helpful dreams.

Wish Fulfillment Dreams

Most of us have dreams in which we get something we've longed for or that makes us very happy. These wish fulfillment dreams allow you to psychically experience something you desire and to indulge your fantasies. You could think of them as trial runs that give you a chance to try out a wished-for situation to see how it might work out, before taking a chance in your waking life. Perhaps you're considering changing careers, but aren't sure what path to take. A wish fulfillment dream could let you feel what it might be like doing another type of job. Wish fulfillment dreams can also offer guidance about how to proceed in a situation you feel uncertain about or help you overcome fears that are blocking you from getting what you want.

Wish fulfillment dreams provide insight into your true needs and desires. Pay attention to them. You may not always know consciously what you want—especially if your deepest desires go against what you think you *should* want—but your subconscious does.

Precognitive Dreams

Have you ever dreamed about something than later happened? Precognitive or predictive dreams are less common that the types discussed previously, but many people have them at one time or another. That's because you tap in to the psychic, intuitive part of your mind when you dream, the part that knows no limits in time or space.

Many people say precognitive dreams feel different from ordinary dreams. In some cases, they seem more vivid or immediate. They may progress in a more logical or literal manner, akin to how waking life proceeds, rather than in the convoluted way many other types of dreams unfold. That's not to say a precognitive dream won't speak in symbols, however. I know a woman who always dreams of turbulent water or rainstorms a few days prior to a big argument with her boyfriend. Water is a common symbol for the emotions. Now that she understands her dreams are warning her, she often manages to avoid arguments and find more constructive solutions to problems.

Notice when your dreams come true. Some precognitive dreams prepare you for an upcoming situation. Mark Twain, for example, dreamed of his brother's death and funeral—exactly as it happened three months later. Other dreams, like training films, offer guidance and direction by revealing an outcome in advance. Pay attention to these warnings. Sometimes you'll just get a piece of the message in a dream, and subsequent dreams will add information. If this happens to you, ask your subconscious before you fall asleep to give you the information you need. When you get used to recording your dreams, you'll likely find your dreams predict the future more often than you realized.

Astral Dreams

When you sleep, your mind loosens itself from your body and can freely travel to any place or any time period it chooses. Perhaps the nonphysical part of you is just curious and wants to explore where you can't physically go. Some precognitive dreams may be the result of astral travel. The feeling of *déjà vu*, which means "already seen" in French, could also be rooted in a dream journey to a future time or place.

It's possible you've traveled back into the past in your dreams, too. If you dream of a past event or your dream features clothing, buildings, vehicles, and so on that come from a long-ago period, write down as many details as you can, especially things that you wouldn't be likely to have picked up from books or movies. Then do some research and see if you actually did pick up information from the past.

Connecting with Spirits in Your Dreams

Some people connect with their deceased loved ones in dreams. If you do all the talking in the dream, it could be a sign of mental telepathy; if both you and the other entity communicate with one another, you may actually be meeting a spirit. In Chapter 12, I mentioned that ghosts often appear to us in dreams because we are more likely to accept them in this form than if they showed up in our waking lives. A spirit being may visit you in your dreams to give you a message or to offer love, comfort, and solace.

You can encourage contact with a departed person by programming yourself to meet up with her in the dream state. Before falling asleep, visualize the person you'd like to contact and call her name. Tell yourself that you will, indeed, connect. If you don't succeed the first time you try, don't despair; keep trying. With practice, your skills will improve.

Lucid Dreaming

Have you heard of lucid dreaming? During this type of astral dream, you realize you are dreaming and can manipulate the dream's scenario. If you wish, you can fast-forward the dream to glimpse the future. This lets you foresee what might evolve if you follow one course of action or another. By guiding what happens in your dream, you learn to direct situations in your waking life.

Some researchers recommend trying to see your hands in the dream, in order to become aware of the fact that you are dreaming. This cue is the beginning step to controlling your dreams and the direction they take.

Tips for Remembering Your Dreams

Although we dream several dreams every night, most of us only remember one or two of our dreams—or remember only fragments of them—and some people rarely recall any of their dreams. Unless I'm really focused on remembering my dreams they dissipate almost immediately and I have no memory of them when I awake. It appears to me that people who don't use their intuitive minds much during the waking state tend to have more vivid dreams and sharper dream recall than those of us who engage our intuition and psychic skills regularly. Dreams let us connect with our natural psychic capability and give the intuitive, creative mind an opportunity to establish balance.

My sister Pat is a good example. She claimed she didn't have any psychic ability in her waking state of consciousness. However, she had some extraordinarily accurate dreams about what I did and what was going on in my life. She saw both the present and the future. I felt like she was spying on me in her dreams.

Once she dreamt she saw bugs crawling all over my computer. I immediately ran my virus program and, sure enough, found I had a serious problem. For a while, she kept dreaming about magic tricks with cards. At the time I happened to be dating a magician who did wonderful card tricks, but I hadn't told her about him. One morning she said casually, "I dreamed that you couldn't find your bed." Well, I hadn't slept in my bed; I had spent the night with my boyfriend. You can see why I wanted desperately to stop her from dreaming about me!

Why don't some people remember their dreams? Lack of interest may be the main reason. Physical exhaustion or mind-altering substances in the body, such as alcohol and drugs, can also interfere with dream recall. With a little practice, though, you can improve your dream recall and gain the benefits dreams can offer. Here are some suggestions to help you remember your dreams more clearly.

1. Keep a dream journal. Each morning, as soon as you wake up, record your dreams and date them. This tells your subconscious that you consider your dreams important. Getting into the habit of writing down your dreams stimulates your memory. All dreams have meaning—don't discount ones that seem insignificant or silly. Keeping a journal also lets you see which of your dreams are precognitive, and what messages they want to share with you.

2. If you remember several dreams, record them in order. The progression may be significant.

3. Program yourself to recall your dreams. Before falling asleep, tell yourself that you will remember and understand the meanings of your dreams.

4. Discuss your dreams with others, if you feel comfortable doing so. Sometimes talking about your dreams can prompt your memory. Hearing another person's dream experience might spark a recollection of one of your own dreams. Sharing your dreams can also help you to bet-

ter understand their meanings. One night I had a dream about chipped dishes and plates. When I analyzed it with a friend of mine who was interested in dream interpretations, he suggested I was not eating right—and of course he was right.

5. Keep a pencil and notepad on your bedside table. How many times have you awakened during the night and remembered a dream, but by the time morning comes you've forgotten it? Simply jotting down a few notes about the dream's fundamentals or theme can help you recall the whole thing later on.

6. Drink a lot of water before going to bed. This causes you to wake up during the night and gives you a chance to record a dream while it's still fresh in your mind. If you wait until morning, some dreams may vanish.

7. Meditate. Meditation, which is the art of listening with the ego subdued, breaks down the barrier between the conscious mind and the subconscious. It improves the clarity of dreams and dream recall. Because meditation slows brainwave frequencies from the rapid beta level of waking consciousness to an alpha rate that's closer to sleep, you might remember dreams during meditation.

Deciphering Your Dreams

During the daytime your subconscious records the images you see, the sounds you hear, and the sensations and emotions you experience. At night it processes these experiences and plays them back to you, but in symbolic language. In this way, dreams serve as a bridge between the conscious and the subconscious minds.

Edgar Cayce, who was known as the Sleeping Prophet, said, "All dreams are given for the benefit of the individual, would he but interpret them correctly." Both Freud and Jung believed all dreams offer information that can be useful to us in our waking lives. Here are some tips to help you decipher your dreams.

1. Relate the dream to something that happened during the day. Most dreams are your subconscious mind's attempt to process recent experiences. A conversation with a friend, a TV program you watched, or something you read may spark an idea tucked away in your subconscious. The dream is bringing it up for further examination.

2. Consider your dreams as a series. You usually have three to five dreams per night, and all those dreams might relate to the same problem or topic. The symbols, however, may be different, and you might not realize the various dreams are all trying to emphasize a single, important point. If you think of them as parts of a whole, they could make more sense. The full meaning of a dream can never be found in one symbol. The sum total must be studied, along with the likes and dislikes of the dreamer.

3. In most dreams, every character represents a facet of you. Even the bad guys show sides of you that you have probably repressed or rejected.

4. Consider all the elements of the dream: the setting, people, animals, weather, buildings, plants, actions, words, feelings, colors, and so on. Also examine the condition of the objects

in the dream. For instance, water represents the emotions. Ice—frozen water—suggests cold, hardened emotions.

5. Before you go to sleep, tell yourself that you will understand the meaning of your dreams. If you had a dream in the past that you didn't understand, ask to have the dream again in a form that will be easier for you to interpret.

6. Dreams usually offer advice or guidance. Look for a lesson, information, or warning in a dream. Although the lesson may be presented in a humorous or enjoyable manner, most dreams aren't intended as a form of entertainment.

7. Do you have the same dream over and over, night after night, or perhaps periodically over a span of many years? Maybe the dream's drama changes, but the theme is essentially the same. Recurring dreams indicate your subconscious is trying really hard to communicate to you something that it considers important.

Dream Symbols

We dream in symbols because we tend to think in symbols or pictures at the conscious level. If someone mentions your wife or husband, you immediately picture a human face rather than the word *wife* or *husband*. If I say to you "seventy-two" you'll most likely see the digit 72, not the words. Now notice what happens mentally when you read the word *elephant*.

But because dreams speak to us in symbols, pictures, and puns, we often find them baffling. Understanding what your dreams mean lies in being able to interpret the symbols they contain. As I see it, dreaming is entering a world that uses the language of the subconscious, a language of symbols, signs, and imagery. Messages are sometimes couched in verbal and visual puns. If you dream of being all wet, for example, it could be a visual pun.

To further complicate matters, symbols mean different things to different people. For example, Ann may develop hives whenever she eats strawberries, whereas Barbara enjoys eating them and experiences no ill effect. To Ann, strawberries will be a warning symbol in a dream, but not to Barbara. Different cultures see symbols in different ways, too. Therefore, understanding the cultural context can be valuable in dream interpretation.

Signs and symbols, nonetheless, mean exactly what they say, although we may have to adjust our regular, rigid thinking patterns in order to see this truth.

Here's an example. I once dreamed of a married man I knew, and saw an empty birdcage. I thought perhaps he had lost his bird—a strictly literal translation—but when I asked him he said no, he didn't have a bird, much less a birdcage. Later I learned that he felt trapped, "caged" by his unhappy marriage.

If you are open to them, your dreams will tell you a great deal about yourself, the people you know, and your life situations. Dreaming is one of your most valuable intuitive skills, and one that's readily available to you every night.

Common Dream Symbols

Some symbols show up widely in cultures around the world, both now and in the distant past. For example, circles traditionally symbolize wholeness, and crosses represent the intersection of spirit and matter. Certain symbols appear regularly in many people's dreams, and they mean more or less the same thing to most individuals in most instances. Of course, all of us have our own pet images and associations, which is why a list of universal symbols won't apply to everyone in every case. Here are some of the most common dream symbols:

- Houses represent you and the different areas of your life. The basement relates to your subconscious, the ground floor to your daily life and personality, the attic to your spiritual or mental realm. Pay attention to the details and condition of the house and its features; they describe the nature of your life. A basement crowded with old junk may mean your subconscious is full of outworn attitudes or patterns from the past. A run-down house might indicate you need to do some personal renovation work.

- Cars or other vehicles symbolize your movement through life. Notice the condition and type of vehicle, as well as who's driving it. If someone else is in the driver's seat, you may be allowing another person to steer you along rather than following your own path. Also consider the road you're on—is it steep, rough, winding, smooth? Are you poking along or in the fast lane? Look around and see if you can tell where you're going—the dream could be guiding you in a particular direction.

- Water signifies your emotions. What's your relationship to the water in the dream? Are you swimming in it? Sitting on the shore? Looking down on it from a high bridge? Is the water murky or clear? Smooth or turbulent? Deep or shallow? These images show how you experience your emotions.

- School dreams or dreams of taking a test describe your feelings about your abilities. Many people dream of being late for class or unprepared for an exam, which indicates feelings of inadequacy. However, you might dream of acing a test or graduating from school with extra credit.

- Finding yourself naked in a dream suggests you feel exposed or vulnerable. Notice where you are and how other people in the dream react to your nakedness. These indicate the parts of yourself about which you feel uncertain, but may wish to express.

- Death or dying in a dream usually symbolizes a transition of some sort, not physical death. Something in your waking life may be passing away. If another person dies in the dream, ask yourself what that person represents to you, and consider that in relation to you and your own life. The death of a strict teacher might mean you are becoming less judgmental and more accepting.

- Sex dreams show you are uniting different parts of yourself (or want to). What does your partner in the dream represent to you? His or her qualities—strength, courage, kindness, creativity—are ones you seek to incorporate into yourself.

- Monsters or villains indicate parts of yourself that scare you. What does the monster/beast represent to you? A bull might symbolize sexuality, a shark ruthlessness. How do you react to the monsters in your dreams? Do you run and hide? Consider facing up to them or fighting back and see what happens. Or, better yet, try befriending the bad guys.

- A baby signifies something new is emerging in your life, or the beginning of a new phase or endeavor. This dream might also indicate creativity or fruitfulness. If you dream of a baby animal, consider the qualities you associate with that animal to interpret the meaning of the symbol.

Personal Dream Symbols

Each of us also has a whole set of personal dream symbols that are unique to us. Gerald, for instance, associates peaches with cancer because his mother, who died of cancer, craved peaches during her final illness. For some people, a dream about a horse might represent freedom or movement—but if you're afraid of horses, the dream could mean something entirely different to you. When deciphering your dreams, these individual symbols can be more important than the commonly accepted ones.

Dream Association

Freud popularized a technique of dream association that may help you understand the symbolic language of your own subconscious. He suggested taking one dream symbol and associating it with something in your waking life. Once you make a connection, associate that with something else and continue, seeing what "clicks."

For example, in a dream you might find yourself at the foot of a mountain and feel apprehensive about climbing it. As you discuss the dream, you may realize you've always been afraid of heights. Taking this further, you might make the connection that you feared striving for great heights because you might fall/fail, and this fear has prevented you from achieving your goals. Work your way back through your life in this manner to understand the full meaning of your dream.

Create a Dream Dictionary

To sort out and interpret your own personal symbols, create a dream dictionary. Write down the symbols you notice in your dreams and the connections you make to them in waking life. For instance, you might associate apples with health. One night you dream about eating an apple and enjoying its sweet, juicy flavor. In this case, the apple could indicate you are nourishing yourself in some way. In another dream, though, you bite into the apple and find a worm. This dream could be telling you to pay more attention to your diet or to some other aspect of your life that isn't healthy.

Also note the situations in your dreams when that symbol appears. Is the apple so high up in the tree that you can't reach it? Is it lying on the ground, rotting? Does someone else pluck the apple from your hand before you can eat it? All dream details have significance. In time, and with practice, you'll come to understand this form of psychic communication you have with yourself and learn to use it to guide your life.

CHAPTER RECAP

Everyone dreams every night, although we don't always remember our dreams. However, most dream researchers agree that your dreams are the subconscious mind's attempt to communicate important information to you. They come from the intuitive, creative part of your mind and provide guidance, insights, even glimpses into the future.

Dreams use the language of symbols to talk to you, which can be confusing until you learn to decipher your personal symbols. Some symbols mean similar things to most people, but you also have your own set of individual symbols that are unique to you. Each thing in your dream is significant; each thing relates to some facet of you or your life.

If you have trouble remembering your dreams clearly, keeping a dream journal can help improve your recall. Write down your dreams as soon as you wake up, in as much detail as possible. Discuss them with other people, if you like. Paying attention to your dreams and acknowledging their value will help you remember them.

Epilogue

Practicing and developing my psychic abilities in the early years was exciting on a personal level, although it was also a lonely journey. In many respects, it still is. I was and still am a curiosity to some people, as are many of my colleagues who have believed in the value of raising their psychic awareness and intuitive capabilities. As I wrote earlier, life is balance. The rational mind and the intuitive mind, equally trained, offer you a powerful tool.

This is a promising time, and a perilous time. In my opinion, awareness and development of all the mind's capabilities are critical to our nation and our world. We need more people who are willing to delve into the psychic world and to encourage our understanding of it in our everyday world, to the utmost.

As a psychic detective, I believe we need public awareness of what people like me offer in terms of helping humanity. I encourage law enforcement agencies to realize we can help them. I also urge them to realize that turning to us—and/or developing their own psychic abilities—is not a strange or amazing thing to do, but something that can benefit people who are hurting from crimes. Not only can we solve crimes, we may even be able to prevent them from happening in the future.

Can you imagine a population with enhanced awareness? We could train security personnel to spot someone who is very dangerous in an airport, power plant, utility facility, or subway—places of great vulnerability—not just through profile training and mechanical body scans, but also through psychic, intuitive awareness. Military personnel could utilize remote viewing techniques to detect bombs planted on roadways, in shopping malls, and elsewhere to prevent the deaths of innocent people.

The Internet, Facebook, Twitter, blogs, websites, and e-mail have created a revolution in communication in the world. Tens of millions—billions—of people of all ages can now communicate information about themselves and others within seconds. But are we communicating any deeper, any better?

My dream is we will find a way to work with all the modern technology that's available to us *and* with our psychic ability to improve our own lives and the world.

Index

About the Author

With more than three decades of experience working with law enforcement agencies, psychic investigator Noreen Renier has earned the distinction of "the most credible psychic out there" by Court TV online. She has worked with law enforcement agencies in thirty-eight states and six foreign countries, and provided information in more than 600 criminal cases, which helped lead law enforcement authorities, crime victims, and distressed individuals and families to successful conclusions.

The first psychic to ever work with the FBI, Renier has taught at the FBI academy in Quantico, Virginia. She continues to work as a psychic investigator and lives outside of Charlottesville, Virginia. You may contact her at *www.noreenrenier.com*.

.

6077124R00147